DEEP INDIGO

DEEP INDIGO

Lady Dorothy D'Oyly Carte and
St. Yves de Verteuil in Tobago
1933–1978

Elizabeth Cadiz Topp

Cover photo: Courtesy of Harriet Fraser
Author photo: Courtesy of John Cadiz

Issued in print and electronic formats.
ISBN 978-1-7773427-0-8 (paperback).-- 978-1-7773427-1-5 (EPUB).--
ISBN 978-1-7773427-2-2 (Kindle)

This is an original print edition of *Deep Indigo*.

TO BOB

Contents

Prologue — 1

Introduction — 3

1   In Which Lady Dorothy and St. Yves Misbehave and Cause Scandal in the Family — 6

2   St. Yves and Sabine in England, and a Disaster at Sea — 12

3   St. Yves Grows Up in Trinidad and Goes to School in England — 17

4   St. Yves Is Away When a Double Tragedy Strikes the de Verteuil Family — 25

5   Dorothy's Gilded Childhood and Her First Marriage — 29

6   Gilbert and Sullivan and The Savoy — 35

7   A Side-Trip into the World of Psmith and P.G. Wodehouse — 39

8   St. Yves: Ambulance Driver in World War I — 42

9   Dorothy and Rupert Living the High Life — 47

10   The Death of a Son, and a Crumbling Marriage — 54

11   Dorothy's Love Affair with Tobago — 58

12   Twenty-Seven Miles Long, Eight Across — 63

13   The Titled English Lady Takes on A.P.T. James — 69

14   The de Verteuils Learn to Love Dorothy, Corn-bird Hat and All — 80

15   The Grande Dame of Tobago Leaves But Cannot Stay Away — 85

Addendum I   Trip Diary — 95

Addendum II   Dorothy's Homes — 102

Addendum III   Dorothy's Will — 103

Prologue

The story you are about to read is a true one. It takes place in the islands of Trinidad and Tobago in the years before Independence, gained in 1962.

There are two protagonists in this story, a man and a woman, both white, and both the products and beneficiaries of British colonialism.

One, St. Yves de Verteuil, was a Trinidadian of several generations back, of noble French ancestry, who worked all his life in the senior ranks of the British civil service in Trinidad. The de Verteuil family was well known in the island. They were descended from Chevalier Michel Julien de Verteuil, who, with the essential labour of enslaved people of African ancestry, had established himself as a cocoa planter late in the eighteenth century.

The other was an Englishwoman, Lady Dorothy D'Oyly Carte, née Gathorne-Hardy, an aristocrat of relatively new vintage, from a family that had made its money in the iron furnaces of Yorkshire, and later benefitted from close historical connections to both Westminster and the British monarchy.

Lady Dorothy and St. Yves were both from the upper echelons of their respective groups, one built on the subtle stratifications of birth, wealth, accent and education, and the other on not so subtle layers of skin colour, from dark at the bottom to white at the top.

What fascinated me about this story was how Lady Dorothy, with St. Yves at her side, was able to overturn the strictures placed on her by her position at the top, and to enter fully and productively into the rich and multi-racial life of Tobago. She was a remarkable woman, powerful, generous and eccentric, and it has given me enormous pleasure to try to bring her to life in these pages.

Introduction

Growing up in the Trinidad countryside in the 1950s, I lost myself in books, one of the few legitimate amusements available to me, and a welcome escape from the chaotic household of eight siblings in which I was number four. A dedicated reader, I was not a particularly choosy one. And as puberty set in, Little Women and Little Lord Fauntleroy gave way to tales of penniless young women whose lives were changed by the love of a man who was hard to get but very handsome and charming and rich. This is what got my imagination firing, as I read at night under the mosquito net in the bed that I shared with my younger sister, who did not appreciate being kept awake by my flashlight glowing under the top sheet.

These tales always involved a rescue, from a world of want and limited prospects, into one of extraordinary privilege, luxury and power. The heroine moved, Cinderella-like, from the first world into the second and infinitely more desirable one, and of course lived happily ever after, dispensing philanthropy, being really nice to those who had wronged her in her first life, and adoring her sensitive and handsome prince, while they produced a crop of beautiful children.

This penchant for the princely was fed by another minor current, that of family stories. I can't speak for my father's background, knowledge of which is mired in the archives of Venezuela, a country which currently has more important matters to consider than where the Cadiz family sprang from. But my mother's antecedents are well documented, and her family tree bristles with former glory, with 'de la' this and 'du' that, the tiny French *particules* which suggest that your family came from the nobility. De la Chancellerie, de la Falaise, de Gannes, de Verteuil, Dupont de Gourville, lords and seigneurs, chevaliers and barons! This was the stuff that I loved to listen to, living as we did on our father's barely adequate salary, in our bare-bones, ranch-style house built without the aid of an architect, with tree frogs living in the lavatory tanks that flung themselves at you every time the toilet was flushed.

Our house was built on land given to my mother by her mother, who was the daughter of Gaston de la Chancellerie de Gannes and Sophie Cipriani (of Corsican stock, who brought to the marriage her considerable wealth). The land had once been part of a cocoa estate, on which Gaston and Sophie had built La Chance, a three-storied wooden house with ten bedrooms and great floor-to-ceiling mirrors in the drawing room which reflected and multiplied the glittering brass lamps with their glass shades hanging above.

All that was left of La Chance when we moved there were the stately royal palms that lined the driveway, a few old footings, and the stories my mother told me. Her aristocratic past was just that – the distant past, a collection of fragments, with nothing tactile or tangible, nothing that added up to anything really, the last shreds of the traditions that her European forebears brought with them, of no importance.

It was inevitable that given this background of romantic musings I would be unable to resist the story that you are about to read, of how a titled aristocrat, one with many tangible assets indeed, came into our family for real and set the Cinderella fable firmly on its head. She was the tall, dark and handsome one, born to high status and means, heiress to a gilded life few of us can dream of, and she gave it all up. She lived for the rest of her life an ocean away from her grand homes, her titled family and her very rich husband back in England.

That is what financial independence and the confidence born of an upper-class upbringing could mean for a woman almost a century ago – the power not to wait on the favour bestowed by the kiss of a prince, but the power to change the narrative, to find her man, embrace him and kiss him firmly on the mouth. The more I unearthed about this foreign bird of bright plumage who landed so confidently on a branch of my family tree, the greater the necessity I felt to tell her story, and that of the man with whom she shared her life in Tobago.

Chapter 1

In which Lady Dorothy and St. Yves misbehave and cause scandal in the family

The notice on the inside page of *The Times* of London was small and easy to miss among all the competing news of the war, but for the upper strata of English society it was of considerable if somewhat prurient interest. It was December 18, 1941, and Rupert D'Oyly Carte, owner of the D'Oyly Carte Opera Company and of the legendary Savoy hotel, Claridge's, The Berkeley and of Simpson's in the Strand, in short, a very rich and well-connected man, had been granted a divorce from his wife of thirty-five years, Lady Dorothy Milner Gathorne-Hardy, daughter of the Earl of Cranbrook. Spicing up the legalese was the startling fact that to facilitate the divorce, Lady Dorothy had provided Rupert with evidence of misconduct, an adulterous affair in which she had engaged at her villa in Tobago, West Indies. The co-respondent was one St. Yves de Verteuil. Who on earth, society asked, over its morning coffee, is this man de Verteuil? Of what sort of family? Is he a gigolo, a fortune hunter? And what, pray tell, is the colour of his skin? In other words, is this going to be a scandal diverting enough to provide some relief from a London deep into the deprivations of the Second World War?

Lady Dorothy D'Oyly Carte. Try saying it in a Caribbean accent. It has a rhythmic quality, with the three consecutive 'ee' sounds followed by the soft 'Carte' ending, and would make a great first line of a limerick. I chanted it repetitively as a child, until told to stop. I picked it up no doubt while eavesdropping on my parents and their friends as they sat in the early evening at our house in Arima, Trinidad, the porch hung with fern baskets, its view of the Northern Range growing quickly darker as the sun set. In those grown-up circles, the drinks trolley was trundled out, Vat 19 rum poured with a thick shot glass onto ice cubes and sloshed with Cannings soda water, cigarettes lit, Crix crackers and cheese passed around, while the frogs bellowed in a chorus loud enough to drown out conversation, which only got louder as a result. At cocktail hour, children were tolerated only if useful. We skulked around the perimeter like a pack of dogs, ran errands, took orders ('Can you see what on earth that barking is about?' 'We need more ice'). And we listened.

The Lady Dorothy–St. Yves story, whatever it might have meant to London society, was a scandal in Trinidad, but for entirely different reasons. St. Yves was no gigolo. In fact, he was a close relative, and a widower in his sixties. He was our mother's uncle. The very thought of him being sexually active at somebody's villa was enough to make us gag on our Crix. And by conducting an adulterous affair, the scandal of which was compounded by making it into the newspaper, St. Yves was engaging in behaviour which ran contrary to the tenets of the Roman Catholic Church, and the de Verteuils of Trinidad were deeply Catholic. The couple, although they got married shortly after Dorothy's divorce, in a civil ceremony, were still considered to be 'living in sin' and their union could not be sanctioned until they were married by a priest in the Catholic Church. And this could not happen until the death of Rupert D'Oyly-Carte, by no means imminent. They were the cause of scandal. Visits with St. Yves and Dorothy would have to be surreptitious, in the hope that no-one else would drop in while they were there.

People 'dropped in' in those days, randomly, and if no-one was at home because they were dropping in on someone else, you just trolled around in your car until you found the welcoming lights of a house. This was usually done between five and seven in the evening. Our mother would be sure to get out of her gardening clothes and be showered, dressed and lipsticked for this nightly ritual. Dad would arrive from work, march down the corridor to his bath, and while dressing would often see the headlights of a visiting car coming up the road. This was greeted with vile curses, because what he really wanted to do was putter before dinner on the wooden cabin cruiser set on trestles in the backyard which he hoped to launch one day. But once in his after-work outfit of shorts and fresh shirt, back down the corridor he would march, arms outstretched, kissing and shaking hands with a double grip, assuring his guests that they were the very people he had hoped would drop in.

And had the adulterous couple visited us, they would have been welcome on our porch. I can't be sure that they ever did, because they were living a distance away in Tobago and our house was far enough from the centre of the action in Port of Spain that most of our drop-ins were local Arima people. But Mum in particular would have loved seeing her favourite uncle, St. Yves, and Dorothy would have charmed her. Our parents were not scrupulously 'by the book' when it came to religious teachings. In fact Dad was a sceptical Anglican and stayed home and cooked eggs while we were spruced up and trotted off to Sunday Mass at the Santa Rosa Church in Arima. On the odd occasion when he did accompany us, if one of us was making our First Communion for example, or getting confirmed, he could be quite embarrassing, announcing *sotto voce* when the Sanctus bells rang that someone should answer the phone, or pretending to help himself to the collection plate.

But for other more observant relatives, it was a problem, and one not alleviated by the fact that Dorothy was titled, a 'Lady' in her own right, and very high in the social stratosphere. The reason this cut no ice was because the de Verteuils too felt themselves to be no mean family, and were not interested in absorbing an aristocratic 'Lady' merely to enhance their social position. The de Verteuils were not rich at all, like they had been back in the day when they were prosperous wine merchants in Bordeaux and the French King Henry IV of Navarre bestowed on them titles (Baron de Feuillas) and other marks of nobility, like a motto (*Post Nubila Phoebus*) and a very grand coat of arms (three red lozenges on a silver background). Their faithful allegiance through the centuries to the royal cause meant that for generations back their sons were all officers in military service, then the exclusive preserve of noblemen. The cost of education in military colleges and then of commissions led to the trickling away of their wealth and the neglect of their land holdings while their men were away on campaigns. This history of absolute loyalty to the King led them to be entirely on the wrong side of the French Revolution, dispossessed and almost completely destroyed, chateaux and farms razed to the ground during the Reign of Terror and the counter-revolutionary War of the Vendée (1793). In one of life's strange serendipities, a surviving son of the family, Chevalier Michel Julien, was able to escape to England, and having survived countless adventures, each of which could have killed him, washed up like a coconut on the shores of Trinidad in 1797, rooted himself there, and established a thriving plantation of de Verteuils and of cocoa.

de Verteuil family gathering, c. 1900 (St. Yves encircled)

So in a contest of who was more noble than whom, and for how long, the de Verteuils would win hands down. The blood that ran in their veins had matured over the centuries to a deep indigo, compared to Lady Dorothy's pale shade of robin's egg blue. Dorothy's background, wealth and social position would not be enough to overcome their strong antipathy to divorce and to her marriage to St. Yves.

The couple therefore made the wise move of starting their life together not in Trinidad but in the nearby sister-island of Tobago, an overnight ferry away from raised eyebrows and disapproving looks. Dorothy already owned a charming villa there, designed by herself, and the scene of the adultery. She named her villa Ridgway after her mother, who before she became Countess Cranbrook, was Cicely Wilhelmina Ridgway. It sat on a hill, surrounded by sixty acres of forest and garden, near the fishing village of Plymouth, overlooking a Caribbean coast scalloped with beaches and aerated by the most delicious warm breezes.

Did their relationship begin as an affair between two irresponsible people, carried on at Ridgway in the sultry tropical nights, all tangled sheets and mosquito netting? And if it did, how did it morph into marriage? They were fourteen years apart in age, he sixty-seven, she fifty-three. She was born to grand homes and gardens staffed by nannies, butlers, maids, cooks and gardeners. Winter holidays abroad, to Crete and Madeira, fine restaurants, and expensive cars were standard fare, and she mixed in a social circle of equally upper-class and important people in London, the centre of the English-speaking world. He in contrast came from a large French Creole family of fluctuating means, long rooted in a small Caribbean island of such insignificance that few in England had ever heard of it. He had worked all his life in Trinidad, in the British colonial service. He was retired and living on a government pension. He was Roman Catholic, she was Protestant. She was taller than he was. They were in many respects from starkly different worlds. But her marriage had been crumbling for a decade, and his wife had died in a terrible disaster at sea. He must have been astonished to find her. She was fresh, new and unimpeded. She represented a hopeful future. They were both wounded, and available and open to each other. Despite all the fuss about Dorothy being a divorcée, they made the bold decision to start a new chapter together. And so they went to the Warden's Office in Scarborough, the main town of Tobago, and Lady Dorothy D'Oyly Carte became Lady Dorothy de Verteuil.

Chapter 2

St. Yves and Sabine in England,
and a disaster at sea

When he met Dorothy, St. Yves was recently bereaved. He and his wife of many years, Sabine (née Sellier), had left Trinidad in the late summer of 1939, taking the 'long leave' which was a valued perquisite to colonial civil servants, allowing them three months to return to the mother country. St. Yves was at the time the warden of St. George county in north-west Trinidad and thoroughly Trinidadian, generations back, with no family connection to England at all. However, long leave applied to all colonial civil servants of a certain rank, British-born or not, and Sabine and St. Yves decided to make use of it. In hindsight, an England about to descend into the maelstrom of the Second World War might seem a foolhardy choice for an extended holiday. But Prime Minister Chamberlain was engaged in appeasement talks with Hitler that had convinced the British public that promises of peace would indeed hold true. In August, despite the crush of German troops on Poland's borders, Chamberlain saw fit to head north to Scotland for a few weeks of salmon fishing. It was only when the announcement came that Germany and the Soviet Union had signed a non-aggression pact that no-one, not even Neville Chamberlain, could deny that Europe was going to be hurled into war, which was declared by the prime minister on the wireless at 11.15 on a sunny Sunday morning, September 3, 1939. Sabine and St. Yves were witness to sandbags piled in front of government buildings, boarded-up store windows, and soldiers and police at tunnels and bridges on the lookout for saboteurs. Searchlights pierced the night sky in a London otherwise completely devoid of light after nightfall. Blackout curtains were mandatory, and wardens patrolled the streets to be sure that not a sliver of light escaped. Slit trenches were dug in the leafy parks, and cellars and basements requisitioned for air-raid shelters. Every citizen was issued a gas mask, smelly, rubbery things with small mica eyes. Barrage balloons, tethered on cables, floated high above the city. It was time for Sabine and St. Yves to leave an increasingly dangerous England and to go home.

They specifically chose a neutral ship, the SS *Simon Bolivar*, for their return journey, as it was owned by the Royal Netherlands Steamship Company. Early in the war, the Netherlands had adopted a policy of strict neutrality in contrast to England and France, countries openly at war with Germany. St. Yves and Sabine travelled across the English Channel to board the ship at the Dutch port of IJmuiden. They embarked at night, and once on board, inspected their cabin, checked their luggage, and walked around the ship a bit before heading for bed. There were four hundred people on board, and a significant number of children. Many of the passengers were Jews heading for South America, fleeing the dawning horror of Nazi persecution. People chatted away in English, German and Dutch, and St. Yves and Dorothy were among a group going back to their homes in the West Indies, which included his nephew Ian de Verteuil, who had just completed his engineering degree in the U.K.

Saturday, November 18, 1939, the first day at sea, was gloomy, foggy and damp. After breakfast, a band began to play to entertain the passengers. St. Yves went out on deck to get some air, and Sabine went to the front of the ship, to the smoking lounge. At about 11.45, this placid shipboard existence was rent by a catastrophic explosion. Those on deck were thrown against the floor with such force that they were unable to move at first.

Children screamed in panic. The decks were covered in blood and dead bodies. The captain of the ship, up on the bridge, was killed instantly, and radio communication knocked out. There had been no time to rehearse safety procedures, so the survivors wandered in a daze, some with shards of glass embedded in their bodies, in their necks. Crew members lowered whatever lifeboats were accessible. But within a mere fifteen minutes, there was another, even more violent explosion. This time the boiler room was hit, and black oil spewed everywhere, covering faces, hair, bodies. Some jumped into the water as the ship sank fast, in a hissing mess of steam and oil. But as they reached the water, the waves hit with extreme force, and swimming was almost impossible because of the thick layer of oil and the dragging effect of oil-soaked clothing. Clinging onto floating debris was the only hope. The *Simon Bolivar* sank to the bottom of a sea so shallow that her two funnels remained clear of the water off the coast of Harwich for several years, like a child's toy in a bathtub. Three German destroyers had mined the English Channel on November 17, the day before, and the *Simon Bolivar* was destroyed by two magnetic mines. These mines – as distinct from the more familiar floating contact mine (the one with spikes) – lie in wait on the sea bottom. A ship passing tens of metres above distorts the earth's normal magnetic field enough to trigger the waiting beast.

St. Yves was not with Sabine at the time of the explosion. He found himself in a lifeboat unable, amidst the utter confusion, to find her. His nephew, Ian, ended up in the sea and was pulled from the cold waters of the English Channel after several hours, covered in black oil. He was rescued by one of the seven ships, most of them Royal Navy, who came to the scene. Survivors were taken to London on passing ships, and some to nearby Harwich, where they were housed at the Parkeston Railway Hotel, presenting a strange sight, covered in grease and oil and sodden clothing, among the starched linen and silver of the hotel dining room.

THE SINKING OF THE DUTCH LINER "SIMON BOLIVAR" BY A GERMAN MINE: SURVIVORS FLOATING IN A SEA OF FUEL OIL.

Sinking of the Simon Bolivar by G. H. Davis
© *Illustrated London News Ltd/Mary Evans*

One of the most remarkable escapes was that of a father and his three-year-old daughter, whom he saved by putting her in a wooden box he found on deck, pushing it into the water, and swimming behind it for nearly an hour before being rescued by a minesweeper. Sydney G. Preece told a newspaper reporter that during the whole time his child behaved remarkably. She was not at all perturbed and bobbing on an oily sea in her little wooden box, asked him, 'Are we going to Trinidad in this, Daddy?'

There was, however, no comic side to St. Yves and Sabine's situation.

We know that she did not die immediately of her injuries, as a cable was sent to the de Verteuils in Trinidad on November 19, the day after the explosion with the news that they were all safe.

But she did not survive for long and died a few days later, one of eighty-six lives lost. One can only imagine the desolation suffered by St. Yves, who, having barely survived himself, and still coping with the shock and horror of his ordeal at sea, had to bury his wife in England before making his way back to Trinidad. (The family was told that her grave is in Felixstowe, but a concerted effort by the volunteers of the Felixstowe Museum to find its location has been without success.)

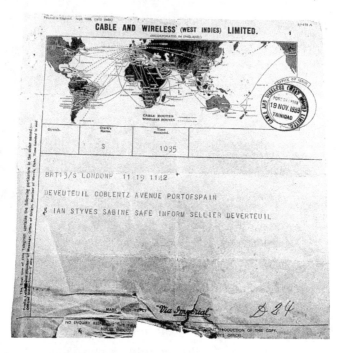

Sixty-four years old, St. Yves was close to retirement from his wardenship. He had a decent government pension, and he and Sabine had no children. As Britain headed inexorably into world war, he headed back home to Trinidad and to what he thought would be a quiet, lonely retirement.

Chapter 3

St. Yves grows up in Trinidad and goes to school in England

I did not know him at all, my great-uncle. He was said to be a charming man, very well mannered and easy to be with, if rather given to quoting Shakespeare. He also had a reputation of never exerting himself overly much, so some would say was well suited to the colonial civil service. On the other hand, he had impressed the British government enough to have been awarded the M.B.E. (Member of the Order of the British Empire) in 1932, and that same year was appointed by the governor to a five-year term as an unofficial member of the colony's Legislative Council, the local governing body.

St. Yves was the youngest, the *lagniappe* (surprise baby), in a family of twelve, ten boys and two girls. His mother Elisa, my great-grandmother, forty-five at the time of his birth in 1875, treasured this beautiful child. His early life was spent in rural Trinidad, where his father, Louis Julien, managed a series of large sugar estates for their absentee British owners. The estates employed indentured labourers, brought to Trinidad by the British colonial government from India, to alleviate the labour shortage resulting from the emancipation of slaves in 1834. The Indian workers' children were playmates for the young de Verteuils. Elisa, being the manager's wife, was fortunate to have a number of household servants to help her: a cook, maid, laundress, nanny, handyman and yardboy. In a letter to her son Ferdinand, who was studying medicine in Ireland, Elisa writes of them: 'Concord [the name of their estate in central Trinidad] has not changed since you left. Massa, Chasury, Gollies, Elizabeth and Agnes are still here. Bissoo sends you a handshake'. Louis Julien and Elisa were eventually to buy Concord from the owners, Tennant and Company, a brewing firm in England.

For the older children, secondary school meant leaving Concord and staying in Port of Spain at the family's house, under the supervision of grandmother Bonne, while Elisa remained in the country with Louis and the younger ones. School holidays were spent at a holiday home on Monos, one of a string of small islands stretching between the north-west tip of Trinidad and the mauve hills of Venezuela far away on the horizon. 'Ma Toquade' (My Whim) sat on fifty-eight acres of forested hillside on a narrow strip of level ground fronted by a fine shingle beach known as Anse Caribe by the fishermen, two of whom, Mathieu and Cestoute, were resident on the island and spoke only French patois. A hired barge took them to Ma Toquade, unloading not only the family and household staff, but also a cow for ready milk, a suckling pig and a cage of chickens. A wide gallery ran along the front of the house, shaded by jalousie windows and filled with rocking chairs.

Ma Toquade, the de Verteuil holiday home on Monos

Visitors and overnight guests were frequent. There was a lot of singing and card games, and of course Anse Caribe provided endless bathing in the satiny warm green sea. The occasional humpback whale put on a show, flinging itself into the air and down again with a mighty splash, mimicked by its calf.

These idyllic holidays would come to an end, in the nature of idylls, when it became clear that Louis Julien could no longer fight the malaria that had afflicted him sporadically for years. He became fatally ill with this disease which was endemic in Trinidad, spread as it was by the mosquitoes which flourished in the countryside during the rainy season. Louis went to Ma Toquade one last time and stayed for as long as possible, until there was no delaying a return to Port of Spain. He died surrounded by his family, including his four-year-old son, St. Yves.

Elisa was not yet fifty. She was left with a large family to raise and educate, and she was not a rich widow. She was forced to sell Concord and moved with the children who were still at home – St. Yves and his two sisters Ange and Blanche – to their Port of Spain house with grandmother, Bonne. St. Yves was the treasured youngest child in a house full of women. St. Yves would leave this cossetted female world when he was sent to boarding school at thirteen, but Ange and Blanche continued to live together until their deaths, never marrying. My mother would visit her two tiny aunts (their diminutive size was thought to be the reason they never married) as they sat on the shaded rear verandah, after their morning baths in the austere concrete bathhouse at the back. They would submerge themselves in the cool water wearing white linen chemises, with yolk panels of hand-sewn tiny tucks interspersed with lace, and then sit, soaking wet, fanning with large straw fans in the tropical heat. A maid brought them iced mangoes and oranges on a wooden tray, as the breeze gently dried their chemises and they chatted with my mother.

Going away to boarding school was common practice for children of the colonies. St. Yves was sent to England, to board at the famous Ushaw College, a combined Catholic seminary and school, in the countryside near Durham. Going to Ushaw was a family tradition, and in all there are seven de Verteuils listed in the Ushaw register. It would be my turn two generations later, in September 1957, to go to school in England. I was sent to Notre

Dame Convent, near Lingfield, Surrey – the senior common room overlooked the Lingfield racecourse, and we once saw the Queen strolling around the paddock with her purse. In this flock of new girls were siblings, cousins, friends of cousins. We were twelve years old, verging on thirteen. The convent that my mother and her two sisters had gone to had closed its doors in 1939 (the property is now the Notre Dame Housing Estate in Clapham). A new convent school had to be found for us. It was run by sisters of a different order, the School Sisters of Notre Dame. The Mother Superior, Mother Hildegarde, was American from the Midwest, with a soft, lined face and an outward severity which was a cover for a kind and gentle heart. We never saw anything but her face and hands. The rest of her was locked into a starched white wimple and a black habit, a rosary with beads the size of quail's eggs around her waist. Sometimes a wisp of hair would escape from under her wimple, a small transgression. The only physical contact we had with the nuns was a hand touching the waist or up on the shoulder when they taught us how to ballroom dance. The wimple was then pulled back and pinned in great white wings at the back, leaving a glimpse of the neck covered in a white cotton fitted hood. The nuns came from all over, the U.S., Canada, Belgium, Ireland, Germany, England. They must have been a little bewildered by this sudden influx from the Caribbean. We didn't drink tea, so they provided morning coffee. We were always cold, so they taught us how to layer our bedclothes, and to put our uniform shirts and tunics between the layers at night so they wouldn't be too icy cold in the chilly mornings. They treated our chilblains with a feather dipped in warm oil. An elocution teacher was hired just for us. Miss Isobel Derry pronounced that we would never be accepted into the 'better homes of England' unless we learned to speak without our Trinidad accents, with their stresses on all the wrong syllables, and so began a regime of reciting passages from *Winnie-the-Pooh* and other texts to prepare for the annual R.A.D.A. (Royal Academy of Dramatic Art) exams. In addition to learning to speak like the Queen, a skill as quickly lost as it was gained, we became proficient in the Scriptures, passed a few G.C.E. exams, and some of us attempted the A-levels, but there was never any thought given to going on to university or to any form of professional training that might gain us a job any more ambitious than being a secretary. No-one encouraged this, and none of us became competent at anything outside of the domestic sphere. What the nuns hoped to produce instead were modest, deferent and considerate young women, taught to value others over themselves. My sister Marie Louise became very interested in joining the nunnery, but our sceptical father put that idea to rest by insisting that she wait until she was twenty-one, by which time she had married an American navy man and was living in New Jersey nursing the first of their five children. While in England, she and I were fortunate to fly back and forth to Trinidad for the longer holidays on free airline tickets, our father being at that time the chief engineer for B.W.I.A. (British West Indies Airways). We made the trip, all twenty-four hours of it, leapfrogging from London to Reykjavik, then to Gander, Bermuda and Barbados, twice a year, at Christmas and then for the summer holidays.

Marie Louise, our mother Rosemarie, and me, en route to England, 1955

St. Yves, generations earlier, would never have gone home during the five years he spent at Ushaw. Maybe he was invited to spend Christmas at the home of a school friend, and Elisa no doubt made arrangements to keep him occupied during the summer holidays. Also in contrast to my experience at school in England, he was getting one of the finest educations the country could offer. Ushaw was housed in massive Georgian buildings facing a quadrangle, around which had sprung up chapels, a library, an infirmary, a hall, kitchens and farm buildings. Several of the more important buildings were designed by various members of the famous Pugin family of architects in their trademark neo-Gothic style, with the vaulted ceilings, pointed arches and polychrome decoration an interesting contrast to the more sober Georgian style of the earlier buildings. The senior Pugin, Augustus Welby Northmore (his most famous project the interior design for the Houses of Parliament), was responsible for the 1847 chapel in which St. Yves would spend many a cold morning at Mass; his son E.W. Pugin designed the refectory where St. Yves was introduced to the boarding school cuisine of north England, and Peter Pugin, who had himself attended Ushaw, was responsible for the Junior House where St. Yves spent his first years. He had grown up in wooden-planked, high-ceilinged, airy houses ringed with verandahs. Now his days were spent in grand, echoing stone spaces lined with carved and gilded panelling, with heavy stone fireplaces and miles of tiled corridors. His tropical linen and cotton clothes were exchanged for heavy wool and serge, stout shoes and wool socks.

The womanly milieu of his childhood gave way to a stern, exclusively male world. The only women he would ever see regularly would be chambermaids or kitchen workers. He was taught entirely by men. Ushaw had an idiosyncratic curriculum. His first class was known as 'Underlow', and he progressed through Low Figures and High Figures. He then entered the college proper, and learned Grammar, Syntax, Poetry and Rhetoric. At the end of each term, an event known as 'Reading Up' took place in the Exhibition Hall. The students of each year, known as a 'school', were lined up on the stage facing the teaching staff and the assembled college. A lecturer then announced in Latin the position of each student in the Latin examinations. As each name was announced, starting with the first, the student returned to his seat, leaving his less successful colleagues waiting to hear their fate, until the last one made his humiliating way back to his place.

St. Yves at Ushaw, c. 1887

Another of Ushaw's idiosyncrasies was that the College had its own game, played nowhere else, somewhat like quidditch at Hogwarts, although of course, as any Harry Potter fan will tell you, quidditch is played both professionally and at other wizarding schools. The Ushaw game originated in Flanders and was called 'Cat', from the French *quatorze* or fourteen, this being the number of players on the ring in the 'bounds' or sports field. The striking team carried a 'cat-stick' made from ash, and the feeder team lobbed to the strikers a wooden ball covered in hot pitch, cotton tape and plaster.

Among those who excelled at Ushaw, not necessarily at Cat but certainly at classes, were future cardinals, like the great scholar Cardinal Wiseman, eminent historians, John Lingard for example, High Court judges and attorneys-general, statesmen and military officers, artists, architects, authors, including the poet Francis Thompson, author of "The Hound of Heaven" (1893), and Joe Tasker, one of Britain's most talented mountain climbers, who started climbing in Ushaw's quarry. We can imagine St. Yves in the middle of the pack, as he was evidently able enough to survive at Ushaw for his entire secondary school education.

Chapter 4

St. Yves is away when a double tragedy strikes the de Verteuil family

Elisa was a widow struggling to survive financially when St. Yves was at Ushaw. Where did she find the money to send him there? And why did she consider it so important to do so? Some of her older sons had gone to St. Mary's College, a fine day school and just down the street from her home in Port of Spain. Why did she think it wise to send her youngest so far away, and for so long? We can only guess that she did so on the advice of other family members, who were perhaps able to help finance St. Yves's education. (The price of cocoa took a sharp rise in the last quarter of the nineteenth century, leading to a welcome surplus of cash for the French Creole planters.) But perhaps also it was to protect him from the overwhelming sadness about to engulf the family with the deaths in 1887, when St. Yves was twelve, of his two older brothers within weeks of each other, Gaston, aged twenty-seven, and Maxime, twenty. The brothers had been suffering for several years from the dreaded disease, leprosy, as it was called then. Dr. Gerhard Armauer Hansen of Norway discovered its cause, the Mycobacterium leprae, in 1873, and it is now renamed Hansen's disease and is highly treatable. But this came too late for Maxime and Gaston. Only humans and certain South American armadillos get leprosy, and how they get it is uncertain, but the most likely cause is that the germ is spread by coughing or sneezing. Their early symptoms were benign, not a cause for concern. A persistent rash perhaps, light patches on their suntanned skin. There might have been a bit of numbness in hands and feet, and inexplicable breakouts of blisters. Leprosy starts slowly and gestates for a long time. Their symptoms would have slowly worsened. The hands and feet grown weak. Limp wrists, dropped feet. Strange thickening of the ears and the face, painful nodules, an inability to close their eyelids.

For Gaston and Maxime, the options were very few. Their uncle, Sir Louis de Verteuil, a medical doctor, wrote in 1857 that leprosy was on the increase, and that parents should pay strict attention to cleanliness and open-air exercise. An asylum was established at Cocorite, on the outskirts of Port of Spain, for lepers who could not support themselves. Cocorite was considered a place of terror, given the primitive medical treatments of the time and the crude skills of the underpaid wardens. The Cocorite leper asylum was not a place for Gaston and Maxime.

Elisa and Louis Julien tried everything from a list of limited options, in an era when medicine had little to offer. They made the long pilgrimage from Trinidad across the Atlantic to the Roman Catholic shrine at Lourdes, deep in the shadows of the French Pyrenees. Here Elisa prayed for a cure at the spot where Our Lady was reputed to have appeared in 1842 to a fourteen-year-old asthmatic village girl, Bernadette Soubirous. During one of the appearances, Bernadette was instructed by the Lady to scratch at the ground outside the grotto. Upon doing so, a small trickle of water appeared which then grew into a bubbling stream. It is in this water of Lourdes that the sick are said to be healed. They immerse themselves in it, and despite the high E. coli count, they drink it; it is bottled and carried around the world. Cures were reported regularly at Lourdes; in fact, by 1908, the shrine's golden jubilee, 3,962 cures had been recorded, reaching a peak of 236 in a single year (1898). Permanent cures are registered in the medical department at Lourdes, called at that time the Bureau des Constatations Médicales, run by a committee of doctors. The Catholic Church was from the beginning hesitant about Lourdes and went to great lengths to ensure that the evidence of a cure would be incontestable, sensitive as it was to claims of superstition, delusion and self-interest. When Elisa was at Lourdes, she was certain that she witnessed a cure, the sudden, miraculous healing of a child at the Grotto. She brought back bottles of Lourdes holy water with her to Trinidad and applied it regularly to the nodules and lesions erupting on her sons' bodies.

Louis Julien, on the other hand, sought a more scientific cure, taking six-year-old Maxime, in whom the disease was not yet advanced, to Paris, to see one Dr. Cazénore, only to discover that the 'doctor' was a quack. He then went to Dr. Bazin, a well-known authority on skin diseases, who held out some hope for a cure, prescribing a special diet and bathing twice daily in mineral waters. Louis Julien was forced eventually to return to work and family in Trinidad, leaving young Maxime in France for four years at the St. Barbes des Champs children's hospital, a seventy-minute carriage ride from Paris. But Maxime was not helped, not by the holy water of Lourdes, nor the mineral waters of Dr. Bazin, and after Louis Julien's death Elisa could no longer afford his hospitalization. He returned from France, in 1881, when St. Yves was seven. Maxime was by then a fourteen-year-old teenager, and a visible leper. On the ship which brought him back to Trinidad, he was considered untouchable and was shunned by fellow passengers. On arrival in the harbour of Port of Spain, they refused to have him join them in the tender taking them to shore. Instead, he was brought, shrouded in white bandages, in the dead of night, in a rowboat manned by a de Verteuil cousin, from the ship anchored in the Gulf of Paria to the Port of Spain wharf where Elisa waited.

Elisa then felt that she had no choice but to isolate Gaston and Maxime at Jouvence, the remote cocoa plantation high up in the forested hillsides of the Northern Range, which had been developed by the Chevalier and which still belonged to the family. Bonne, her seventy-year-old mother, went with the boys to Jouvence, and cared for them until they were unable to walk and she sensed that death was imminent. She brought them back to their home in Port of Spain. Maxime died first, in September 1887, followed five weeks later by Gaston.

Thirteen-year-old St. Yves, in his second year at Ushaw, was protected by distance from this sadness. He would not know about his brothers' deaths until several weeks later, the length of time it would take Elisa to write to him and for the letter to travel across the Atlantic by ship and then by mail-train north to Durham. When, some eighty years later, two of my brothers, Robert, twenty-three, and Peter, eighteen, died in Trinidad, within months of each other, Robert in a work accident and Peter of malignant melanoma, I was twenty-one and already far away studying and working in Toronto. I was notified by long-distance phone calls. I look back on my response at that time. I didn't want to go home to their funerals, so I pleaded lack of funds, not untrue, but I could have easily borrowed the money. Instead, I chose to be away from home at that time, relieved to be protected by distance from the grief engulfing my family so many miles away in Arima. I wanted to stay as far away from it as I possibly could. Did St. Yves, perhaps, feel the same way? Of course he had no choice in the matter, without a Jules Verne balloon. But I had a choice, a Boeing 747, a short five-hour flight direct from Toronto to Port of Spain.

Chapter 5

Dorothy's gilded childhood and her first marriage

Dorothy was also the youngest of a large family, the seven children born to John Stewart Gathorne-Hardy, Lord Medway and the future Lord Cranbrook, and Cicely Ridgway, and was even more of a lagniappe than St. Yves, born in 1889 nine years after her brother Nigel. She was raised as practically an only child, with only her much older sister Jane, lame from infancy and confined to a wheelchair, still at home. Their London address was the first house built in the new residential development Cadogan Square, completed only the year before. The large, red-brick houses were built around the four sides of a central garden, with gates that lock, restricted to residents. Now one of the most desirable and expensive addresses in London, it's hard to imagine how close Cadogan Square then was to the countryside when her family moved there. Her grandfather, the Earl of Cranbrook, lived on Grosvenor Place, near Buckingham Palace, and remembered shooting snipe nearby in Belgravia. Stewart and Cicely and their seven children spent the winters in London, Christmas at his father, Lord Cranbrook's enormous (4,900 acre) estate at Hemsted, Kent, and in the summer they went to The Grange, a property in the village of Benenden, about a mile from Hemsted. Where did all this wealth come from?

When first the shapeless sable ore
Is laid in heaps around Low Moor,
The roaring blast, the quiv'ring flame,
Give to the masses another name:
White as the sun the metal runs,
For horse-shoe nails, or thund'ring guns

...

No pen can write, no mind can soar
To tell the wonders of Low Moor.
(John Nicholson, 1790-1843)

The Hardy family was one of the three founding families of the Low Moor ironworks in Yorkshire. This made them immensely rich. Directed by Dorothy's great-great-grandfather, John Hardy, a solicitor from Bradford, the Low Moor works grew to an enormous scale; in fact they became the largest ironworks in all of Yorkshire, England's industrial heartland. Low Moor occupied a major complex of mines, mountains of coal and ore, kilns, blast furnaces, forges and slag heaps, all connected by a network of railway lines. Dorothy's grandfather, while inheriting the great wealth generated by Low Moor, did not take an active role in the company, a role filled by his brother Charles. Instead he became a solicitor, but then ran for Parliament, embarking on a political career that made him one of the most powerful men in England, holding a series of senior Cabinet positions (Secretary of War, Secretary of State for India, Home Secretary) in the Tory governments led by Benjamin Disraeli and later by the Marquess of Salisbury. He would be honoured in 1892 by Queen Victoria with the title of Earl of Cranbrook. He was a trusted confidante and advisor to the Queen, with whom he frequently dined and corresponded. Stuck among the pages of Dorothy's copy of her grandfather's biography, which she had in her Tobago library, was a letter from Queen Victoria, thanking Lord Cranbrook for his kind letter of sympathy to her after her favourite gillie, John Browne, died.

Dorothy jotted down in her later years some vivid memories of her childhood. She led a charmed if somewhat solitary life, close to the outdoors, far away from the filthy slag heaps and blast furnaces of Low Moor. There were few children her age to play with, and she had instead a childhood fascination with animals. From the age of eight she had a roan pony, which she rode sidesaddle. Unfortunately, her pony had a condition called 'staggers', and would without warning fall on its knees, sending small Dorothy over its head, mostly unharmed. She also drove two donkeys, a mother and daughter, in tandem, and discovered that if you put daughter donkey in front of the mother donkey in the shafts, the daughter was always turning around and licking the mother's nose, which slowed things down.

She was comfortable with very small animals as well and travelled around with a white rat, Spice, which lived in her rabbit fur muff. Cadogan Square is close to Harrods, and the white-coated man at the counter was ready for her daily request: 'Would you mind giving me a biscuit for my rat?' After Spice had babies, she could no longer keep them all in her muff and had to resort to a cage. As an adult, Dorothy was known to keep white mice in her handbag and to play with them on trains, thus guaranteeing lots of room to herself in the compartment.

There was one time in her childhood when Dorothy nearly died, from an illness so serious that prayers were said for her in church. She was ten years old and had contracted whooping cough (or pertussis, now almost eradicated by vaccination). It led to double pneumonia, untreatable at that time. She remembered four doctors standing at the foot of her bed, discussing possible treatments. Straw was scattered around the Cadogan Square house, so that she would not be disturbed by the clip-clop of horses' hooves. She took digitalis in a silver spoon, as her heart was weakening. She was tended at night by an elderly nurse dressed in a very dark red housecoat with buttons down the front, and during the day by a nurse from St. George's Hospital, whom she thought tiresome.

Once over the crisis, and back to her healthy self, she went regularly with her family to Scotland in the summers where she became adept at fishing for salmon, shooting grouse and stalking deer. When indoors, she took great pleasure in fitting out a small three-shelved cupboard with bits of wallpaper and some glue, and making furniture out of matchboxes. And at their country place in Kent, her father gave her two hurdles, some twine and some sacking, and she made herself a house in the shrubbery where she could be happily alone with her collie. This would be a harbinger of a delight and skill in designing and decorating houses of her own, in England and later in Tobago. She also remembered as a child the lovely oak trees and two ponds at their home in Kent and going with her father to Hemsted when he was involved in planting trees and shrubs in the extensive gardens there. Again, her love and skill with gardens became one of her defining enthusiasms.

But while living in beautiful, often grand spaces, staffed with servants, like most girls of her class she was relatively uneducated in the more formal school subjects. Her brothers, like St. Yves, went to highly regarded boarding schools, in their case Eton. She on the other hand never went to school, but was privately tutored at home. Her parents hired various live-in governesses, both English and foreign, whose role was to shape Dorothy into a cultivated young woman who would be as marriageable as possible. The first governess was an Englishwoman whom Dorothy thought rather ancient and prissy, but seeing that she left to get married, she could not have been very old. The second was German, a fine pianist, who beat Dorothy over the knuckles with a ruler when she played a wrong note. This lady unfortunately broke her neck falling off a ladder while on holiday. She was replaced by another German woman, whom Dorothy disliked intensely, and who eventually left, defeated by the child's mad spells of falling on the floor and scratching like a cat at the carpet. Then finally, success: an Irish governess, a fine teacher and superb pianist. She made Dorothy's lessons interesting, guiding her reading and mathematical skills. She would learn to speak passable French, and to play the piano quite well. She did needlework, became familiar with some Shakespeare and poetry, and learned where places were in the world.

Books were also a passion of Dorothy's. Her grandfather, Lord Cranbrook, had an enormous library, and enjoyed reading to his grandchildren. He had a full, low, powerful voice, used to great effect in parliamentary debates. In fact, he was considered to be one of the finest orators of his time. It must have been a great pleasure to listen to him as he brought to life the adventures of Robin Hood and Gulliver, and the Knights of the Round Table. However, upper-class girls like her were not really encouraged to be clever, or overly interested in books. That would veer into the dangerous territory of the bluestocking, a learned and intellectually inclined woman with limited appeal in the marriage market. Queen Elizabeth II, for example, never went to school, but was taught by a governess. Time has brought change, however, and her daughter, Princess Anne, went to the Benenden School for Girls, housed in the Hemsted estate which once belonged to Dorothy's grandfather.

Lady Dorothy's upbringing led to just the right result. She was good looking, tall, dark-haired with regular, strong features; she was from a very rich family with strong political connections; and her father would, on his father's death, become Lord Cranbrook. It took her very little time to meet her first husband. The social season in London began shortly before Christmas and ended in June. It involved many parties, large and small, private and public, at which eligible young people had a chance to get to know each other. The Savoy was a popular place for these events. Was it at one of these parties that young Dorothy attracted the attention of the thirty-year-old Rupert D'Oyly Carte? He was already a highly sophisticated man of the world, and about to inherit his father's business empire. Of slim build, exquisitely groomed and tailored, he was reserved and unflappable in manner, had impressive social skills and a working knowledge of several European languages. He was an excellent yachtsman. She, barely eighteen, was tall, shapely and well-featured, with a head of unruly dark curls. She would be hard to miss and was no doubt very fashionably and expensively dressed and bejewelled.

Lady Dorothy D'Oyly Carte, 1920, portrait by Bassano

She was athletic, fond of swimming, fishing and shooting, but given her background would have had no trouble knowing her way equally well around a ballroom and engaging in appropriate small talk. Rupert and Dorothy met, danced, chatted, and were married within the same year. She had not yet been presented at court as a debutante. Her mother, Cicely, would arrange this shortly after her marriage.

Chapter 6

Gilbert and Sullivan and The Savoy

Rupert and Dorothy's wedding, on June 6, 1907, was something of a sensation, a coming-together of two worlds, Society and Drama, according to the newspapers, which usually didn't mix. It is doubtful that the Gathorne-Hardy family had any previous connection with the D'Oyly Cartes, as famous a name as it was then.

Stage circles just a couple of decades earlier would have been considered distinctly *outré* for an earl's daughter. But it was Rupert's father, the famous Victorian impresario Richard D'Oyly Carte, who had transformed musical theatre and brought new respectability to it. Theatre owners had been regarded as generally shady characters making a precarious living, while playwrights made little money and could survive only by doubling up as actors or journalists. By the mid-1800s, tragedy, comedy and satire had been overshadowed by melodrama, relying on lurid scenes of murder, torture and haunted castles, or by burlesque and pantomime, all quite raffish and risqué. Productions were slapdash, and music sloppily performed. In this demimonde, actresses were thought to be little better than prostitutes. Single men would grab the best seats, to better judge the attractiveness of the actresses on stage. A note sent backstage by an usher would often result in a rendezvous. Not surprisingly, the social elite had effectively stopped going to the musical theatre altogether. Richard D'Oyly Carte recognized that a change was necessary to bring in the monied, middle- and upper-class audience. When he met two very talented young men, the librettist W.S. Gilbert and the composer Arthur Sullivan, his fortune was made. Both had cut their teeth in the world of British comic opera, and Richard D'Oyly Carte was able to get them to agree to work exclusively with him. He was then a theatrical agent, who counted Oscar Wilde and the artist James Whistler among his clients. D'Oyly Carte's ambition was to stage comic opera in a theatre dedicated to the art form, using a repertory company exclusively for this purpose. And so in 1881, he opened the Savoy Theatre, the most modern and glamorous theatre in London, and the first to be lit by electricity. He was a very smart promoter, who made the first nights of Gilbert and Sullivan operas much anticipated events in London's social calendar. Crowds gathered outside the theatre like they do now during film festivals, to ogle celebrities and beautifully turned-out society couples, and the newspaper reviews, generally favourable, led to long line-ups at the box office and the satisfying exchange of money for a night of memorable entertainment.

The essence of the Savoy style, Gilbert explained, was treating 'a thoroughly farcical subject in a thoroughly serious manner', and while superbly musical and entertaining, it was nevertheless scrupulously decorous. There was no cross-dressing, as was common in pantomimes and burlesque, and the women's costumes were entirely decent, no heaving bosoms or exposed thighs. The men's and women's dressing rooms were on opposite ends of the stage, and God help the roué hoping for a quick pick-up. He risked being promptly ejected from the theatre on orders from Gilbert. This insistence on middle-class morals led to the company being nicknamed The Savoy Boarding School. In time, Gilbert would boast that 'we are world known and as much an institution as Westminster Abbey', and the D'Oyly Carte Opera Company, with its repertoire of Gilbert and Sullivan masterpieces such as the still-popular *HMS Pinafore* (1878), *The Pirates of Penzance* (1879), and *The Mikado* (1885), travelled all over Great Britain and overseas, and were rapturously received in the United States. Audiences lapped up the clever lyrics, the light-hearted, hummable melodies, the political satire and outlandish plots laced with strange coincidences, and outsized characters like the Lord Chancellor in *Iolanthe* (1882) and Poo-Bah in *The Mikado*. Gilbert and Sullivan were left by D'Oyly Carte in absolute control of whatever happened on the stage, while he managed the business of their triumvirate. Sullivan drilled and disciplined the orchestra, coming down hard on poor attendance or unenthusiastic playing. Gilbert oversaw the casting, stage design, costuming and staging of the operas, notoriously rehearsing the chorus and principals to the point of exhaustion. The result of this insistence on perfection is that these shows were exquisitely produced and enormously popular, with their music whistled on the streets of London, and belted out while taking one's weekly bath in a tin tub pulled up to the fire.

Proving again his skills as a businessman, D'Oyly Carte decided to build next to the Savoy Theatre a place for out-of-town theatre patrons to stay. This became The Savoy, London's first luxury hotel with electric lighting, elevators servicing the 268 rooms, and marble bathrooms with constantly available hot water. It was the most up-to-date hotel in England. The Savoy! Luxury beyond imagining, where most de Verteuils would not dream of staying on their trips to London, either because it was too flashy or more likely because they couldn't afford it.

D'Oyly Carte hired only the best to run it. The Savoy's first general manager was César Ritz, whose last name has become an adjective, 'ritzy', famously used by Irving Berlin in the song 'Puttin' on the Ritz'. César Ritz oversaw with D'Oyly Carte the positioning of the hotel in the very heart of cosmopolitan London life, as the place for socialites and celebrities, for royalty and the better-heeled bohemian artists and newly minted millionaires, guaranteed to give the hotel the expensive gloss which it maintains to this day, despite the tendency among today's rich and famous to sport sneakers, track pants and tattoos.

To ensure that they came back again and again, Savoy guests were fed by none other than Auguste Escoffier, history's most celebrated cook and the patron saint of professional chefs, known for his tightly run kitchen, several famous cookbooks, and the refining of the five great sauces of haute cuisine: béchamel, velouté, hollandaise, espagnole and tomate.

This fabled partnership came to a crashing end, however, when it was discovered that both Escoffier and Ritz were crooks on a rather grand scale, having over several years defrauded The Savoy of more than three million dollars in today's money. D'Oyly Carte sacked them on March 7, 1898, for larceny, embezzlement and fraud. Disturbances in The Savoy kitchens on that day reached the newspapers, which ran headlines such as 'A Kitchen Revolt at the Savoy'. *The Star* reported: 'Three managers have been dismissed, and 16 fiery French and Swiss cooks (some of them took their long knives and placed themselves in a position of defiance) have been bundled out by the aid of a strong force of Metropolitan police'. Ritz and Escoffier both confessed to having spent the entire eight years of their employment with the D'Oyly Cartes taking kickbacks and a five-percent commission in cash from suppliers who made up their losses by shorting their deliveries. This criminal behaviour was not revealed publicly at the time, and the pair, after signing confessions and making partial retribution, was free to go.

Why did the D'Oyly Cartes not wish to make the circumstances public? Their silence was to their own financial detriment, because Ritz and Escoffier went on to establish Paris' Ritz Hotel and then the Carlton Hotel in London, which soon became a serious competitor to The Savoy. Had charges been laid, it is unlikely that Ritz and Escoffier would have had any commercial success whatever, languishing as they would have been in an insalubrious London jail, eating terrible food with a tin spoon on tin plates.

The matter only came to light nearly a century later, in 1983, when a young trainee accountant, Ian Bostridge, was rummaging through The Savoy archives. It is thought that they kept it a secret because they did not want to upset the ailing and aging Queen Victoria with this scandal. Her son Edward, Prince of Wales, was one of The Savoy's most important clients, and any press enquiry into the Ritz/Escoffier matter could have revealed the extent to which the future king used the hotel to entertain his fifty-five known mistresses.

Chapter 7

A side-trip into the world of Psmith and P.G. Wodehouse

This chapter is by and large a digression, but I ask you to bear with me. I will return to St. Yves and Dorothy in chapter eight. But what I'm about to tell you speaks to the ways in which small links and oblique connections add to the fabric of our lives, giving them dazzle, colour and shape.

Unlike his young, home-schooled bride, Rupert, like St. Yves, had attended a very fine school indeed. Winchester College is the oldest of the prestigious boys boarding schools in England, its ostensible purpose being to prepare students to enter university, which Rupert did, attending Magdalen College at Oxford but leaving after two years to be schooled by his father Richard in the family business. But Winchester's deeper purpose was to nourish the upper classes with a steady supply of well-educated gentlemen, privileged at birth and carefully groomed by the masters to be leaders and to maintain the rigid caste system of English society. It's been said that a boy could be flogged every day of his school life, could never pass an exam, could even be expelled, but at least he could claim to be a Wykehamist, or an Old Etonian, and wear the school tie – a necessary badge of belonging, and as much a marker of social acceptance as being a debutante who was presented at court was for young women.

Rupert was noticed at Winchester by a schoolmate who, struck by the way he carried himself, described him to his cousin, P.G. Wodehouse. 'Rupert … was long, slender, always beautifully dressed and very dignified. His speech was what is known as orotund, and he wore a monocle. He habitually addressed his fellow Wykehamists as "Comrade", and when one of the masters chanced to inquire as to his health his reply was: "Sir, I grow thinnah and thinnah"'. According to his biographer, Benny Green, Wodehouse was so taken by this description that it inspired one of his great comic creations, Psmith, introduced to the world in 1907, the year in which Rupert and Dorothy got married. Psmith appears in the first of the 'Mike' series of novels by Wodehouse: 'A very long, thin youth, with a solemn face and immaculate clothes, was leaning against the mantelpiece. As Mike entered, he fumbled in his top left waistcoat pocket, produced an eyeglass attached to a cord, and fixed it in his right eye. With the help of this aid to vision he inspected Mike in silence for a while, then having flicked an invisible speck of dust from the left sleeve of his coat, he spoke. ... "My name ... is Smith ... if ever you have occasion to write to me, would you mind sticking a P at the beginning of my name? P-s-m-i-t-h. See? There are too many Smiths, and I don't care for Smythe ... in conversation you may address me as Rupert (though I hope you won't) or simply Smith, the P not being sounded"'. In *Psmith, Journalist* [1915], he expounds upon the pronunciation, 'Compare such words as ptarmigan, psalm, and phthisis'.

For Wodehouse, 'the character of Psmith is the only thing in my literary career which was handed to me on a platter with watercress around it, thus enabling me to avoid the blood, sweat and tears inseparable from an author's life.... Jeeves and the rest of my dramatis personae had to be built up from their foundations, but Psmith came to me ready-made'.

Rupert was not as 'long' as Psmith, and didn't wear a monocle, but he did have a rather formal and cool demeanour. Whether his speech pattern could be described as orotund we don't know, nor is there any indication that he was pleased or not by being so immortalized in a series of comic novels that were bestsellers in their time and are still in print. One imagines that he took it all with resigned good humour, and that Dorothy got a huge charge out of the whole thing.

But we do know that Wodehouse, in turn, was a huge Gilbert and Sullivan aficionado, knew their comic operas intimately, and had a habit of slipping references to them into his work. He was an especial devotee of Gilbert, that grand purveyor of comic light verse. He was invited once at the age of twenty-one, a 'shrinking floweret', to Gilbert's country mansion, Grim's Dyke, where he infuriated his often-curmudgeonly host by nervously laughing in the middle of an anecdote and spoiling Gilbert's punch line. 'I had rather an individual laugh in those days, something like the explosion of one of those gas mains that slays six, and it lasts for about five minutes, by which time the company had begun to talk of other things, and Gilbert never got to the point of it at all. And it was at this juncture that I caught my host's eye. I shall always remember that glare of pure hatred which I saw in it … His eyes beneath their beetling brows seared my very soul. In order to get away from them, I averted my gaze and found myself encountering that of the butler. His eyes were shining with a doglike devotion … I appeared to have made his day'.

So to climb out of this rabbit hole, great-uncle St. Yves's second wife Lady Dorothy D'Oyly Carte's first husband was Rupert D'Oyly Carte, the inspiration for P.G. Wodehouse's famous comic character, Psmith. Wodehouse was a huge fan of Gilbert, of Gilbert and Sullivan, the partnership whose series of comic operas were produced and staged by … Richard, and later by Richard's son, Rupert. And so the world turns, circles within circles, barely skimming, often colliding, and so intriguing to disentangle when they do.

Chapter 8

St. Yves and Dorothy during the years of the First World War

The glamorous D'Oyly Cartes, beloved by social columnists, settled upon their marriage in 1907, into their first home on their very own private island in the middle of the Thames, sixteen miles from Charing Cross. When Rupert's father, Richard, bought Folly Eyot, as it was then known, it was wooded, irregular in shape, and uninhabited. He planned to use the island as an annex to The Savoy, a retreat for guests to enjoy the tranquil charms of the flowing river. To this end he had built a large, thirteen-bedroom dwelling with a ballroom and gardens. The shape of the island was regularized into an ellipse, with walkways built all around. The plan was that guests would arrive by train at the Weybridge station, ten minutes away. Access to the island was by chain ferry. Richard's plans were however thwarted by local magistrates, who refused him a liquor license, and so he made the island into his private family retreat instead. Rupert inherited D'Oyly Carte Island, and Dorothy became mistress of Eyot House. When not on the island, they lived in central London, at 6 Derby Street in Mayfair, with a lovely walled garden.

Dorothy had little time to adjust to her life with Rupert, however, as she gave birth almost exactly nine months after her June wedding, to Bridget. Michael was born three years later, in 1911. And in 1914, war broke out and Rupert went off to serve in the Royal Navy. It is thought that he also had some sort of secret role as 'The King's Messenger', which involved dispatch cases and unexplained trips abroad, and which drew on his many international connections and facility with languages acquired through the hotel business.

A CHARMING PORTRAIT.

Miss Compton Collier, West End Lane, N.W.

LADY DOROTHY D'OYLY CARTE AND HER CHILDREN

Lady Dorothy D'Oyly Carte is the wife of Mr. Rupert D'Oyly Carte, who, in addition to other activities, is the present proprietor and controlling force of the famous D'Oyly Carte organisation. Mr. Rupert D'Oyly Carte is the younger son of the late Mr. Richard D'Oyly Carte. The D'Oyly Carte company will open with an extended season of the Gilbert and Sullivan operas at Princes Theatre at the end of September. Lady Dorothy D'Oyly Carte is a daughter of the 2nd Earl of Cranbrook

What Rupert did in the war sounds a lot more intriguing than St. Yves's war experience. At the age of forty-one, St. Yves signed up with a contingent from Trinidad, and headed to England for the second time to volunteer as an ambulance driver. He was too old for combat but knew how to drive a car, not a common skill at that time. In fact, he was one of the first Trinidadians to own a motor car. Probably not a steam-powered Locomobile Runabout, the first car ever imported to Trinidad (in 1900), but more likely a Ford Model T, launched in 1908, and the first affordable car, a runaway success for the Ford Motor Company. Henry Ford famously said that a customer could have a car painted any colour that he wants 'so long as it was black'. But in the first years of production, it was available only in gray, green, blue and red. I like to picture St. Yves in a shiny red model, driving goggles on, Sabine beside him hatted and veiled against the dust and wind, the sisters Ange and Blanche in the back seat with their mother Elisa in the middle, tearing around the country roads of Trinidad at 15 miles an hour, tooting the horn to scare away hysterical chickens.

For St. Yves to make the huge personal sacrifice, to leave Sabine and his bright red car, to travel for weeks across the stormy Atlantic in a troop ship to volunteer in one of the bloodiest, most deadly wars in history, can perhaps be explained by the family tradition from which he came. The old aristocracy in France, that of the ancien régime, prior to the French Revolution, was as layered as a mille-feuille pastry. The top layer, the upper crust, consisting of those directly related to the Crown, the princes of the blood; next were the aristocrats who acted as courtiers, advisors and counselors to the King, and lived in Paris or at court, and were 'ducs' and 'marquis'; after that the 'noblesse de robe', the holders of the chief public appointments which were inherited or put up for sale within a few noble families; and finally, the noblesse d'epée. The eldest son of this last layer inherited the title and lands, while the younger sons joined the army or navy as officer cadets. As mentioned earlier, the de Verteuil family had for centuries followed this pattern. The family tree is festooned with the medals of military men; several of them have been awarded the Order of St. Louis for bravery in battle. The founder of the Trinidad family, Chevalier Michel Julien, was an extraordinarily tenacious and brave naval officer; legend has it that he was the first of the British conquering forces to set foot on the muddy soil of Trinidad at Mucurapo when they wrested the island from the Spanish. It is not, therefore, surprising to find that no less than ten de Verteuils from Trinidad volunteered for service in World War I.

At the start of the war, ambulances were horse-drawn, but then wealthy families began donating their cars to the cause, and sometimes their chauffeurs as well. These donated cars were then fitted with ambulance bodies, but with little guidance from the authorities, the result was at first a bizarre collection of hybrid vehicles with no clear guidelines for repairing and servicing. Eventually, the British Red Cross laid down clear specifications, and a measure of standardisation was achieved, making it possible to order ambulances directly from the car manufacturers. St. Yves could have driven a Rolls-Royce, a Daimler, a Morris or a Vauxhall among others, with a long, box-like body mounted on the chassis, two swinging doors at the back, and three stretchers on the floor held in place by braces. A large red cross was painted on each side, and one on the top, a small measure of defense against being blown up by war planes. His uniform was khaki with, just above the elbow, a white armband sewn on with a large red cross, and in his kit, a tin cup and plate, a steel helmet, and a gas mask. Reflecting the need to free up more men for combat, women drove ambulances too. If this were a novel, and I were Ernest Hemingway, I would have the young Lady Dorothy meeting St. Yves over a stretcher on a gutted field in France. Hemingway was an ambulance driver in World War I, along with many other authors, poets and artists. He drew on this experience for *A Farewell to Arms*, in which the main character is wounded and falls in love with a British nurse in an Italian hospital. But in reality Dorothy already had two young children and was not in a position to exchange her tea-gown for a khaki uniform, and of course, there was Sabine, waiting in Trinidad for St. Yves. He was back home one year later, on a medical discharge, but fortunately with all limbs and faculties in place.

And what did Sabine make of St. Yves taking off like that, to volunteer as an ambulance driver? I wish I knew. I regret very much not being able to bring Sabine to life in these pages. I would love to know what she looked like. How did the life of a warden's wife suit her? A warden was a person of some authority and status within the community, and with the position came a house, a car and chauffeur, and an entertainment allowance. Colonial governors were in the habit of packing foreign visitors off to the wardens who would arrange nature expeditions and visits to local sites, and no doubt Sabine helped with this aspect of the job. It could be a strenuous life, entailing often difficult travel on rough roads, but an engrossing one, as the on-the-ground representative of the Crown. Did Sabine enjoy the relative limelight, of maybe opening a village harvest festival, or giving out medals at school functions? And what did she do, childless as she was, to occupy herself when St. Yves was away in the countryside, inspecting forests and roads, meeting with farmers and hunters, making judgements in the magistrate's court? Did she tend orchids and feed the hummingbirds, and look forward to him coming home in the dusk of late afternoon? Did she play bridge with the local ladies, join committees for worthy causes, and entertain house guests from Port of Spain on the weekend? Or was she deeply bored, did she drink too much and spend a lot of time away in town with her family and friends, leaving St. Yves to fend for himself in the evenings? We will never know; those secrets lie buried with their owner in a grave somewhere in Suffolk.

Chapter 9

Dorothy and Rupert living the high life

When Rupert returned from war service, he and Lady Dorothy continued the glittery life of the society couple, frequently mentioned and photographed in the papers.

Dorothy payed close attention to her public profile, and there is a large leather-bound scrapbook in the Gathorne-Hardy family archive with her press cuttings carefully pasted in page after page, up to the time when she left England for good in the late 1930s. She is described variously as a good driver and fond of the outdoors; as clever, gracious-mannered, able and charming. In November 1921, she and Rupert were on a committee for a Gilbert and Sullivan Ball, to be held in January in the two ballrooms of The Savoy to raise funds for the British Drama League, founded in 1919. 'It was decided to have dancing in both ballrooms, and at midnight the Cachuca, from the Gondoliers, will be performed by members of the D'Oyly Carte Opera Company', reads a press report.

Being a rich upper-class woman entails certain social responsibilities, like supporting your husband's business enterprises, practicing philanthropy, and entertaining and being entertained. A photograph in her scrapbook of Dorothy in a formal gown and tiara on the stage with the Gilbert and Sullivan cast and management after a performance, young Michael in an Eton collar standing at her side and Rupert gazing down protectively at them from the back row, suggests that this was not her favourite thing to do. She looks rather bewildered and out of her element, too big in the shoulders, too tall, in contrast to the pretty soubrettes around her playing so artfully to the camera.

On the stage with Gilbert and Sullivan cast at the Princes Theatre;
Rupert, back row, fourth from the left; Dorothy, middle row, third from right;
standing at her left shoulder, her young son, Michael © Illustrated London
News Ltd/Mary Evans

But being rich also offers the precious luxury of choice. If one chooses to take up sailing, or fishing, or skiing, there are no impediments to doing all those things, and to inviting any friends along that you wish. Having young children did not cramp Dorothy's style at all. They were largely looked after by Mouse, the nanny, and they pop in and out of a diary she kept in 1920, a slim black notebook in which she details several weeks of sailing on their yacht, the *Marionette*, with a crew of two, Adams and James. She clearly loved the rough, physical side of sailing, getting soaking wet, fishing for mackerel, scrubbing and painting, getting stuck in the mud, sitting in the stern and smoking a pipe.

She writes about staying up until midnight and talking politics with the crew, with, no doubt, a brandy or two.

She loved the sea: sailing on it, swimming in it and fishing it, a passion shared by Rupert.

Dorothy aboard the Marionette, 1920

For several fishing seasons in a row, they spent months in the Outer Hebrides off the north-western shore of Scotland, on the island of Lewis and Harris. At the Soval Hunting Lodge, which they leased in its entirety, they and groups of invited friends would rough it while fishing for salmon and trout. They had a new yacht by now, the *Grey Goose*, with a crew of four. Dorothy endeared herself to the Hebrideans, sponsoring Christmas parties for children, opening bazaars, giving prizes and involving herself in the life of the community much as she would later do in Tobago. And it is no wonder given her knowledge of and passion for the sea that she was a leading member, from 1924 until she moved to Tobago, of the London Women's Committee of the Royal National Life-Boat Institution, which, with 4,000 volunteer fishermen, provided and maintained the lifeboat service of the British Isles. In 1934 she was appointed 'life-governor', the highest honour it conferred, in recognition of her valuable services to the Institution.

Life became further enriched when, in 1925, Rupert and Dorothy, while sailing in the *Grey Goose* around the coastline of Devon between Brixham and Dartmouth, spied from the deck a small valley, a combe, sloping down to the sea. They decided on the spot that this was where they would like to build a country retreat. The combe was part of a 2,000-acre estate, farmed since the thirteenth century, and fortuitously it was for sale. They hired the architect, Sir Oswald Milne, well known to Rupert as he had designed the entrance and the ballroom wing for Claridge's hotel, part of Rupert's business empire. Milne had been a pupil of Sir Edwin Lutyens, pioneer of the Arts and Crafts movement of the late nineteenth century, which put great value on the close relationship between the house and its landscape. The shale stone with which the house is built was quarried from the lower part of the combe, using a specially built railway track. The design of the house rejects any ornament, and the rooms and corridors are almost austere as a result. Curtains and cushions in Lady Dorothy's former bedroom were done in a black and white fabric designed by French artist Raoul Dufy. There was particular attention paid to modern conveniences, like heated linen cupboards, powdered glass tiles in the bathroom (also installed in The Savoy), and a wall-mounted electric bell system for summoning servants. Dorothy could push a lapis lazuli servants' bell mounted in the floor underneath the dining table to get the butler's attention, and there was a wall-mounted internal telephone in the cloakroom, for summoning the chauffeur to bring the car from the outside garage to the house. Amazingly, it took only a year from the first sighting of the property for their country house, Coleton Fishacre, to rise above the green of the surrounding countryside.

Coleton Fishacre, shortly after completion, 1926

It would have revealed itself like a well-crafted play, piece by piece, scene by scene. First the prelude, the narrow-hedged roads that lead to it, the stone-pillared gateway, the long drive past the outbuilding that houses the chauffeur's flat and his charges: a fleet of shining cars, a Bentley, a Land Rover, an open-topped sport car. Then the gradual descent on the gravelled drive between low-walled garden beds thick with acacia, buddleia, camellia and fuchsia, figs, pittosporum and jasmine nightshade, to the front entrance, two-storied, in subtle shades of stone, blank, neither intimidating or not, the polite handshake of a house not willing to show itself too soon. Step through the entrance door onto a central roundel with the carved initials R.D.C. – D.D.C, and the date the house was completed, 1926. The butler directs you to step down into the living room, angled off to the right. There for the first time you get a sense of the next act: the gardens, the flowing stream in its granite canal, surrounded by roses, and way off in the distance, a glimpse of the shining sea. But wait, that comes later. Because first, a warm greeting from tall, effusive Lady Dorothy, dressed in a loose patterned silk, and a formal handshake and glimmer of a smile from the linen-suited Rupert, cigarette in hand, just entering from the terrace. The sound of a cocktail shaker, and the pouring into an iced glass of the first martini of this summer evening. Malcolm Sargent, not yet a Sir, is doodling around on the grand piano in front of the windows, slipping in and out of Cole Porter's 'You Do Something to Me' and 'Let's Do It, Let's Fall in Love'. Guests, some with houses in the area, others invited for the weekend, wander onto the terrace, or into the library next door, where the latest costume designs for *The Mikado*, now in rehearsal, are laid out. People talk, exclaim, greet, kiss. Dinner is announced. It is informal, served both in the dining room on the extended table with its deep blue scagliola top painted to look like the sea, and nearby at a separate table in the open loggia. The dinnerware is Italian majolica, again with Rupert and Dorothy's initials intertwined. And after three simple courses, served by the butler and two junior servants, we are invited to tour the gardens in the light of the slowly setting sun. And that is when yet another act begins, vaulting us into a strange twilit magical kingdom, Ariel hovering in the thick bamboos clustering around the waterway, hiding behind the New Zealand tree ferns. The paths lead downward to the sea, and there are glimpses of a small rocky island lying dreamily offshore. Jack Sharland, head gardener, is off in the distance, on a slope, checking on a newly planted shrubbery before heading home to his nearby cottage. Yucca, bromelia, protea and echinacea. The Tree of Heaven, Ailanthus altissima. The Tulip Tree, three trunked, candelabra shaped. The gigantic gunnera like a monstrous rhubarb, unfolding its massive leaves. Billowing swags of hydrangea, pale blue flowers echoing the pale blue sea. Rhododendrons, Chilean fire trees, dogwoods. Plants gathered on holidays in Madeira and Crete, plants purchased from seventy different English nurseries: over ten thousand specimens, all listed in Rupert's plant book. Enchanted and becalmed, the group's chatter slows down and dies out as we stand at the end of the path on the cliff overlooking Pudcombe Cove. Below us is the salt-water swimming pool, which fills and empties with the tides. We absorb the view of the sea, gently swelling in the fading light. And then it's time to join again the world of clever conversation, boozy banter and dessert.

Both Rupert and Lady Dorothy were deeply involved in the design and planting of the gardens. The property benefits from an exceptional microclimate, being south-facing and enjoying the humidity provided by a rill. Included in the plantings therefore are some very rare species from countries as far away as Chile and China. And so the garden was a mixture of native flora left to grow freely and more exotic specimens such as the vast Persian ironwood tree and succulents from the Canary Islands, among her favourite roses and hydrangeas. The couple's beloved Dalmatians and Cairn Terriers roamed freely, and weekend guests had their choice of tennis, shooting, riding, fishing or swimming in the private cove. Those with an interest in gardening could help with the weeding, should there be any left to do, as the D'Oyly Cartes employed six gardeners. And a butler, housekeeper, housemaid, cook and chauffeur. Lady Dorothy lived full-time in the summer at Coleton Fishacre, with Rupert coming for weekends. When in London, she continued her life of social engagements and charity work, and was called on often to join Rupert at theatre events.

This charmed life of a wealthy and popular couple, surrounded by servants, with connections to both the world of theatre and to the hermetic inner circle of the English upper class, seems the stuff of television dramas and glossy magazines. We, peering through the fence, are fascinated by the rich and the well-born, their lives fodder for our imaginations, an escape perhaps from what we perceive as our own limited horizons. But then their son Michael died, and in an instant everything changed.

Chapter 10

The death of a son, and a crumbling marriage

Michael D'Oyly Carte was twenty-one, a heart-breaking age to die. He was a beautiful young man, tall and elegant, with his father's polish and athletic like his mother, beloved of both of them and full of promise. He was in line to take over from Rupert the running of his hotel and theatre empire. To that end, he had been taking a course of hotel training in Germany and was headed south to work for a time in Monte Carlo. It was October 24, 1932. He was driving with a friend, Richard Basil Snagge, and on a winding road between Lenzburg and Aarau in Switzerland they collided with a motorbike. Michael was at the wheel and died instantly. Richard survived with minor injuries, while the driver of the motorbike, a young Swiss workman, died later in hospital. Michael's death was thought by those who knew them well to be the beginning of the unravelling of the D'Oyly Cartes' marriage.

Grieving parents – there is no singular word for them, like 'orphan' or 'widow' or 'widower', and yet it is surely the grief most keenly felt. Among them, the experts tell us, the divorce rate is highest. What a cold, hard fact, and how dreadful that such a loss, and the pain of anger, sadness and guilt that it incurs, can lead to a further loss, the erosion of a long relationship. No letters or witnesses survive to tell us what happened to Dorothy and Rupert, so I must speculate. Were they not able to mourn together? Did Rupert, the product of a very rigorous and disciplined schooling, a taciturn and deeply private man, not want to talk about Michael, while Dorothy desperately needed him to do just that? We know that he felt the loss deeply. Martyn Green, an actor in many D'Oyly Carte productions, writes in his book *Here's a How-de-Do* that 'the heart dropped right out of him. His interest in both the operas and the hotel seems to fade away'. Did Rupert and Dorothy disagree on what to do with Michael's clothes, his letters, his books? And did they to some extent blame each other for Michael's love of fast cars? Dorothy was a keen and reputedly fast driver. And Rupert had incurred the displeasure of the courts more than once. He was fined £3 for driving at 19 miles an hour in 1902, and the following year he was prosecuted for knocking down and injuring a child while driving at 24 miles an hour. According to the papers, he made 'every provision for the comfort of the child', who recovered from the accident. For Michael's twenty-first birthday, he received from his parents the gift of an MG; it was in this car that he died some months later.

Some say that sorrow always comes in threes, and for Dorothy, this proved true. Her mother, Cicely, Countess Cranbrook, to whom she was close, had died shortly before Michael. And Bridget, their older child, was in the middle of a very messy divorce which placed a severe strain on the extended Gathorne-Hardy family, with which Dorothy had close ties. Bridget had married her first cousin, John David Gathorne-Hardy, in October, 1926. He was the third Earl of Cranbrook, and she assumed the title of Countess.

The marriage was ill-conceived. It is thought that the two mothers, Dorothy and Lord Cranbrook's mother, also named Dorothy, had encouraged the marriage. Bridget and Jock (as he was referred to by family) were frequently together as children and had formed a close bond. The forging of these two prominent families, the Gathorne-Hardys and the D'Oyly Cartes, once again created great interest in the press. The social columnist of the *Daily Express* wrote: 'I adored the new "Mikado" dresses of the Gilbert and Sullivan season. But, despite their gorgeousness, my eye kept wandering to the front of the dress circle. There, in the very centre, sat the pretty young bride of Thursday week, Bridget D'Oyly Carte, with her fiancé, the very nice-looking Earl of Cranbrook. Her green scarf was flung over the balcony's edge. They were certainly duly chaperoned, for though her mother, Lady Dorothy, was in a box, she had with her not only her mother-in-law and grandmother-to-be, but also her governess...' And about the wedding itself, the *Evening Standard* wrote, under the headline 'Women Rush a Wedding – Awning Torn Aside at St. George's Church', that the crowd outside the church, made up largely of Gilbert and Sullivan enthusiasts, rushed the church doors and the verger had to be helped by the ushers to keep them at bay. 'As both the gallery and the body of the church were full, the crowd could not see the bridal procession, but they refused to go away until the police had forced their way to the steps leading to the gallery. The noise must have penetrated to the clergy reading the service. An official of the church said he could not remember seeing such an uncontrollable crowd'. Attending the wedding were dukes and duchesses, earls and countesses, many sirs and their ladies, lord abbots and bishops, but all of their good wishes combined were insufficient to save what was a doomed union from the start, and the marriage lasted only four years.

They were young (Bridget was only eighteen, same age as Dorothy when she married Rupert), and sexually incompatible; this we know from a diary that her husband John kept. His sexual appetite exceeded hers, and she was frightened by his demands. After the divorce, Bridget dropped the title of countess, went back to her maiden name, and buried herself in dance and acting classes at the progressive Dartington School, a half-hour drive away from Coleton Fishacre. She would never marry again.

Bridget and Jock at Coleton Fishacre, c. 1926

At Coleton Fishacre, Dorothy's thirty-five-year marriage with Rupert was also coming to an end. Rupert began to sleep in his own room, at the far end of the hall, and spent more and more time in London, where he purchased a flat, known only to himself, for his extramarital affairs. Dorothy began what became annual winter trips to Trinidad and Tobago. She had much to escape from.

Chapter 11

Dorothy's love affair with Tobago

*The water began to lose its grand ocean tint of purple and
deep indigo ... probably owning to the violence which the
Orinoco pours into the Gulf beyond Trinidad. We first
sighted the mountainous outline of Venezuela on the
starboard side, and Trinidad appeared faintly on the left
with islets between.*

– Trip diary, Viscount Cranbrook, 1885

She was not the first of her family to be attracted to these islands. Her
parents, Stewart, Lord Medway, and Lady Cicely, had joined her
grandfather, Gathorne Gathorne-Hardy, then Viscount Cranbrook, on
a five-week trip through the West Indies in 1885. They were
particularly intrigued with Trinidad and Tobago, and afterwards
Cicely always kept a bowl of flamboyant seeds from the Royal
Botanical Gardens in Trinidad in her sitting room, which Dorothy
remembered handling as a child. It was a trip that must have been
spoken about often by the family, and Dorothy tucked it away in the
back of her mind, planning to go there at some time. And then, there
on the hall table of Coleton Fishacre, in 1932, landed a fresh copy of
the magazine *The Field*, in which a Commander Cyril Alford had
written an article on Speyside, Tobago, where he lived with his wife,
Kitty. This article so intrigued her that she persuaded Rupert to travel
with her to Tobago in 1933, and they were guests of the Alfords. It
would be a distraction from their sorrow at Michael's death, and
might heal the rifts beginning to show in their marriage. It was a long
ocean trip to Trinidad and Tobago, two weeks, but it could be a very
pleasant one if you travelled, like they did, first class and in style on

the *Colombie*, the pride of France's Compagnie Générale Transatlantique, and very much to the demanding taste of the owner of The Savoy. Launched at the height of the Depression, in 1931, the *Colombie*, named after one of the countries she would regularly visit, Colombia, was a beautiful intermediate-sized ship, with black hull, white upper decks and two red funnels, and was fitted out with the finest woods and fabrics of the Art Deco period, all guaranteed to present a deluxe image of France. There was a generously sized marble swimming pool for the first-class passengers: Dorothy would have enjoyed this. After stopping at Guadeloupe, Martinique, and Barbados, the D'Oyly Cartes disembarked in Trinidad and then made their way by island ferry to Tobago.

On her next visit to Speyside, Dorothy was alone. She spent three weeks in this remote fishing village in January 1934. There she hosted a moonlight picnic on the beach, cooking over a glowing coalpot while inside her rented bungalow a gramophone spun out a thin stream of popular songs, with the window ledge acting as a bar. After supper a bonfire was set alight on the beach, and everyone went swimming at midnight. Much ink was spent by the social columnists on the comings and goings of this charming titled lady and her friends. Their enthusiastic coverage was carefully cut out of the newspapers and pasted in her scrapbook.

The winter of 1936 found her again in the islands, and again alone, attending a large party at the Queen's Park Hotel in Port of Spain. 'Refreshments were served in one half of the room, the tables being beautifully decorated with pink anthurium lilies, and dancing was enjoyed on the rest of the floor space, music being provided by the Jazz Hounds Orchestra', writes the *Trinidad Guardian*. I searched the printed guest list in vain, hoping to find St. Yves among the people that she met. The names were mainly English, with a smattering of French ones – de Pompignan, Pollonais, de Boissiere. After this grand party, Dorothy left, with her companions the Darrells, for a stay at Caledonia, one of several small islets which dot the passage between Trinidad and

Venezuela, and on which moneyed Trinidadians holiday at their weekend homes. Near to Caledonia was Monos, the island on which St. Yves had spent months of his early life at Ma Toquade. I was very sick on one of those islands, Huevos, closest to Venezuela, owned, then and now, by family friends. I had contracted measles and ran a high fever. Huevos was offered to us as a place of quarantine. I had to stay indoors in those airy, wooden rooms with jalousied windows, away from the bright sunshine. I loved having my mother all to myself at Huevos, a rare treat when one of eight children. The measles rash went into my eyes, but I escaped lightly, not suffering the fate of childhood blindness, of which it is a leading cause. I was born too soon for the measles vaccine, only developed in 1963.

I mentioned Dorothy's travelling companions, the Darrells. Rupert travelled with Dorothy to Trinidad and Tobago only once, in the winter of 1933/34. On later trips, she was accompanied by friends, principal among them the Darrells, Josset and her daughter Audrey. Josset, a former soprano in the chorus of Gilbert and Sullivan operas, was an old friend from the early days of Dorothy's marriage to Rupert. Tall, big-boned and blonde, she was a widow, her husband having died from wounds suffered during World War I. Josset was charming, exuberant, and unconservative, loved giving and going to parties and was partial to a drink. On the dance floor of the Queen's Park Hotel, she was notable in a gown of lime green with a sash of deep, glowing wine red. On a trip with Dorothy in 1937, they stopped in at St. Lucia, and it was there that Josset first saw Pigeon Island, forty acres of uninhabited rock and beach, lying close to the mainland of St. Lucia, a short boat trip or a long swim away. Josset wanted to live there forever, to be the Eve of her own paradise, and Dorothy with her characteristic generosity made it happen, by purchasing for her a 90-year lease for the island. A stone bungalow was built for her, and in time Josset opened up a small bar and kitchen close to the water, The Club, popular with passing yachtspeople. I imagine that Dorothy and Josset visited back and forth, between Tobago and St. Lucia, an overnight trip, at least in the beginning, on the schooners which plied between the islands of the archipelago, accompanied by vendors of fresh produce and pens of chickens, pigs and other farm animals. Regular air traffic between the islands gradually became commonplace in the post-war years. The Australian-born Josset went back to her own name, Legh, married again to a St. Lucian, Tony Snowball, got divorced, and lived to the age of ninety.

Dorothy and Josset Legh c. 1909

Islands within islands. What was Dorothy's fascination with them? Island life, a life in miniature, a microcosm, encapsulating all that a person needs, close at hand. A community of people, all sorts of people from all sorts of backgrounds, but with the common purpose of making life on the island work. You'd better behave yourself on an island; if you don't, you'll be up against a community, and escape is not easy. There is the sea all around you, limiting, controlling, isolating, sometimes frightening. But at the same time, protecting and preventing. An island can be a remote and insignificant place, but it breeds self-sufficient and hardy people and can be home to some of the most interesting wildlife on earth. Dorothy's fascination with islands began with D'Oyly Carte Island in the middle of the Thames, her first home as a married woman. Then Madeira and Crete, for winter holidays with Rupert, followed by fishing holidays on the island of Lewis and Harris in the Outer Hebrides. And finally Trinidad, Caledonia Island, and Pigeon Island, culminating with her most cherished island of all, Tobago.

Chapter 12

Twenty-seven miles long, eight across

Small, simple Tobago. Crisp sand, clear sunlight, curling waves, and along the interior spine, forested hills and deep ravines, filled with all manner of birds and animals: the sabrewing hummingbird, found only in Tobago and in nearby Venezuela, the motmot, with its racquet of tail feathers and iridescent turquoise brow, the magnificent frigate bird, and the rufous-vented chachalaca, known locally as the cocrico because of the sound it makes. Bananaquits and kiskadees, orange-winged Amazon parrots. Anteaters, armadillos, howler and capuchin monkeys, agoutis, eleven species of bat, ocelots and peccaries. Fish teem, and painted pirogues bob at their moorings while sting rays glide in the shallows, floating silently past. Tobago is twenty-seven miles long, eight across, with a population in the 1930s that hovered at fifty thousand, mostly of African descent, unlike larger Trinidad with its riotous mix of Indian, African and Chinese with a dash of Europeans. Unspoiled, underdeveloped, once you get away from the concreted area around the airport, known for its street-side eating places and guest houses.

In 1719, Daniel Defoe shipwrecked Robinson Crusoe on a desert island populated only by wild goats and fierce Amerindians, and gave the literary world its most famous castaway. Crusoe and his major-domo, Man Friday, lived on an island within sight of the 'great island of Trinidad' – and this, according to Tobagonians, could only be Tobago, despite the fact that Defoe's island was a complete invention, he never having travelled beyond the British Isles. He placed his make-believe island at nine degrees north – and therefore south of Trinidad – where no island is. Never mind

– Crusoe's island it remains; there's even a disappointing Crusoe's cave near to the airport that tourists can visit.

In Dorothy's day, there was a Robinson Crusoe Hotel on the windward side of the island, near to the capital, Scarborough. It was a spacious, domestic-looking two-storey building, with a large open area at ground level and a panoramic view of the crashing waves of the windward coast. The thoroughly memorable owners and managers were a Trinidadian brother and sister, Kurt and Vanda Nothnagel, first cousins of my father. Kurt would have been quite at home in a Gilbert and Sullivan comic opera. He was born for the stage. Handsome in a fine-featured, chiselled way, with a coiffured mane of blond hair and shapely legs, he had an inability to shut his mouth, out of which came a steady stream of badinage, delivered in his educated Trinidad accent. He was given to sartorial indulgences, having his swimming trunks tailored for him in England, in cream flannel. These elegant trunks had a woven belt and were pleated at the waist, the costume completed with a large straw hat and a fan, which Kurt waved languidly as he descended into the waves, surrounded by a bobbing of English ladies, emboldened by rum punch and given to much laughter and giddiness. Kurt changed out of the trunks later in the day for a dinner jacket ensemble, hair swept back with Brylcreem like that of a matinée idol. He would sit at the grand piano in the hotel's main room, furnished with Morris chairs slipcovered in cretonne, vases of anthurium lilies on the side tables. Cocktail shaker rimmed with frost, expertly shaken by the white-jacketed bartender. As guests gathered, news of the day was exchanged. Kurt at the piano would take requests. On being asked to play 'There Is Nothing like a Dame', the response was a laconic 'that's what you think, darling'.

And when Vanda (who had been working very hard with her staff all day while Kurt swam with the ladies) appeared on the upper landing, Kurt would burst into a keyboard fanfare, and would then accompany her as she descended in a billowing vestment-like caftan, singing an operatic aria in a reedy soprano. Meals were taken family-style at a large ever-expandable table in the dining room. The Robinson Crusoe attracted the same winter guests, year after year, primarily from England, with Trinidadians going over on the ferry or on the daily B.W.I.A. flights on weekends and during the off-season, when hotel rates were more affordable. Receiving the full benefit of the breezes blowing in from the Atlantic, the hotel was acknowledged to be the coolest place on the island, in a time before air conditioning. Its lounge was used as a sort of informal club by the local residents, giving visitors a chance to meet the local planters, officials and European settlers.

When Dorothy started visiting Tobago in the 1930s, there was one proper town, Scarborough, with some shops, a cinema, many diverse churches, a hospital, a public library, and the Robinson Crusoe, among a handful of small hotels. I would like to think that she drank and dined there, and joined in the shenanigans. There would have been many kindred spirits among the clientele, and this is where I have her meeting St. Yves. He is dapper in his cream linen suit, white shirt and Ushaw tie, dark hair streaked with gray, cut short at the sides and parted. He is sitting at the bar chatting to Vanda while waiting for the overnight ferry back to Trinidad which leaves in an hour. He's in Tobago on government business. He is an unelected member of the Legislative Council and is advising the Tobago cocoa planters, who are having trouble shipping cocoa to Trinidad on the unreliable ferry service. Dorothy comes into the bar with her friends the Alfords, like a galleon in full sail, strikingly dishevelled with her dark hair escaping from under a sun hat. Commander Alford recognizes St. Yves because he had attended a meeting in Speyside which the Turpins, big landowners in the area, had hosted, and at which St. Yves was the guest speaker. They are introduced, St. Yves and Dorothy. She is a bit larger than he is used to. French Creole women tend to be petite, small boned and non-athletic. She has a lovely voice, low-pitched and cultured, and he warms to her curiosity about the island, her confidence and her quick wit. He is a bit of a rare bird to her, as most of her friendships since spending time in Tobago with the Alfords have been with fellow English people. She likes his accent, his excellent manners, and his deep tan. They hit it off. He's only been a widower for a year, after a long marriage, and is rusty in the ways of courtship. He musters the courage to call on her on his next trip to Tobago and asks her to let him know when she is next in Trinidad. They meet like this several times, and of course we know the ending of this story. The relationship deepens and turns to love, until it is time for Dorothy to invite him to stay with her at Ridgway and so provide Rupert with proof of adultery and be granted a divorce.

Which is how it comes to be that Dorothy Milner D'Oyly Carte, divorcée of no occupation, and St. Yves de Verteuil, widower, retired civil servant, are married in the Warden's Office in Scarborough on July 7, 1942.

While this quiet little ceremony was taking place, just the two of them, with three witnesses, the world outside was in turmoil, teetering on the edge as World War II raged on.

In London, Bridget, Dorothy's daughter, had joined The Savoy Group after her brother Michael's death, and with the outbreak of war combined this with child welfare work. The Savoy itself had to cope with bomb damage, food rationing, manpower shortage and a serious decline in the number of foreign visitors. Business picked up however after the Americans joined the war in late 1941 and The Savoy became the favourite of American officers, diplomats and journalists, and a meeting place for war leaders. Winston Churchill often took his cabinet to lunch at the hotel, and Lord Mountbatten and Charles de Gaulle were regulars at the Grill Room where, owing to wartime restrictions, no meal could be more than five shillings. The frequent air-raid sirens sent guests and staff rushing down to the hotel's air-raid shelters in the basement, reputed to be the smartest in London, divided into cubicles, each with a bed and armchair, and staffed by nurses and waiters. Dorothy was of course prevented from visiting or seeing her daughter throughout the war years, as trans-Atlantic travel was very dangerous even if possible.

One interesting anecdote told to me by the archivist at The Savoy is that after the end of World War II, The Savoy Hotel Ltd. decided that it would be a good idea to commission photographic surveys of the main properties in The Savoy Group. In the event of another war, the properties would be fully documented inside and out, and thus could be more easily rebuilt in the event of a future blitz. The photography took place between 1950 and 1951. A complete set of photographs was sent to Lady Dorothy, so that in the event that London was indeed levelled, at least the photographs in Tobago would be preserved to act as the necessary exemplars. But where might they be? They have disappeared, and if ever found, in a box stowed away in a cupboard, or among the many books given away by Dorothy, what will the finder make of them? Maybe recording their existence in this book will be a help, should they ever show up.

Despite rationing and shortage of supplies, Tobago was largely untouched by the war. Nearby Trinidad was in contrast a strategically important military base for the Caribbean, forming the southern anchor of a ring of defenses around the Panama Canal, vital now that the U.S. was engaged in a life-or-death struggle against Japan. There were as many as 135,000 American servicemen at various military bases in Trinidad and 20,000 Trinidadians in the civil defense force – one of whom was my father, sergeant of a platoon in 'Y' company of the Trinidad volunteers, which had its headquarters in a Sea Scouts hut. My older brother remembers the skies filled with fighters and bombers on the way to the American base at Waller Field; of being in a little pirogue heading for one of the outer islands when a huge U.S. submarine surfaced, black and long and mesmerizing; and a massive fire off the docks, where a German U-boat had torpedoed two supply ships. These ships would anchor in the Gulf of Paria, the inland sea between Trinidad and Venezuela, waiting to form convoys before heading across the Atlantic. It was one of these U-boats that destroyed by gunfire a schooner from then-British Guiana in the waters off Tobago; on the schooner were two women and three children who were rescued and then set adrift on a lifeboat which washed up, by a stroke of good fortune, on the Plymouth beach. This was as close as Dorothy would come to the war, as she joined the crowd on the beach to help place the shocked and sick survivors on to a truck which would convey them to the Scarborough hospital, where the matron, Pearl Ottley, her very good friend, was waiting.

Chapter 13

The titled English Lady takes on A.P.T. James

Sometime in the late 1930s, before she met St. Yves, Dorothy had purchased property in the hills near the village of Plymouth, on which she built Ridgway.

A private villa on sixty acres was well within Dorothy's means, her wealth drawn both from her family inheritance and from the divorce settlement with Rupert. But she built Ridgway in a style that was a far cry from the scale and sophistication of Coleton Fishacre. It is a simple, single-storey, three-bedroom bungalow, which she designed herself, with a pitched roof and a front verandah and a small back patio, surrounded by a tropical garden shaded with large trees. But like Coleton Fishacre, it is sited so that it reveals itself slowly, in increments. The long, windy road, quite steep in places, leading up to it is lined with various specimens of large shade trees.

After dropping off passengers, the car can then proceed around the house to park at the back, with the front of the car conveniently facing down the hill. To enter the house, you first walk along a tiled path lined with flowering shrubs and covered by a wooden arbour. The white double-louvred front doors open wide, and as you enter the porch, you realize that while the view from the front is of the solid green of the lawn and the shady trees, the view at the back, from the living room with its high coved ceiling, is of the distant sea, with not a single other dwelling in sight. The sweet breezes of Tobago blow through the house, without interruption.

Ridgway, 2020

Nearby Plymouth, a settlement on the sea, was once the island's principal seaport, and is Tobago's first European community, settled in 1654 by a group of roving Latvians, referred to as Courlanders, then by the Dutch and finally by the British; battle-scarred Tobago was batted around for centuries among various European empires, more so than any other Caribbean island. Plymouth is now a fishing village of a few hundred people. Its long fishing jetty which juts out to sea collapsed many years ago and is still unusable. There are some neat houses on its grid-patterned streets, with swept yards and crotons in biscuit tins lined up along their front walks, and a handful of very low-key historic sites. Behind the village rises the undulating hilly country where Ridgway was built.

A member of the Trinidad cricket team, over to play a match in Plymouth, remembers being served rather generously at Ridgway, and being in very good form that afternoon: 'Lady de Verteuil was lavish in her entertainment and after rum punches we settled for lunch with regular interruptions for whiskey. The whole was topped off with a glass of brandy, and when the game commenced at 2.30 before a generous and appreciative crowd, we were all in high spirits'. The cricketer, Philip Thomson, gives no indication of the outcome of the game, but it would seem that Dorothy had ensured that the Tobago team would have a clear advantage.

Dorothy had always enjoyed an active social life in England, and Tobago proved no different. And of course, St. Yves, a French Creole from Trinidad, had grown up surrounded by people for whom getting together, talking, teasing and laughing was essential to a life well lived. The ability to tell a good story and to make people laugh was a highly prized skill, and a socially awkward French Creole was a rare creature indeed. The 'Plymouth Brethren' was the name given to the group of friends with whom Dorothy and St. Yves played bridge and socialized, and who were considered somewhat 'hoity-toity' by those outside the circle. Perhaps some of them did deserve the appellation, like Anna Short, variously called 'the Countess' or 'the Duchess', a red-haired English socialite whose fame rested on being a stand-in for Deborah Kerr, the English star of the film *Heaven Knows, Mr. Allison*, filmed in Tobago in 1956. Many of these Brethren lived on acreages purchased from Dorothy, whose original holding was subdivided gradually over the years.

Their life was, however, by no means defined by socializing. She and St. Yves became thoroughly embedded in the community around them. We know little about the intimate relationship between St. Yves and Dorothy. For reasons that will become clear later in this narrative, no letters exist, and none have surfaced in Tobago. Very few of the people who knew them well are still alive, and of course there were no children and grandchildren as a repository of family stories. But what I have been able to glean suggests that despite the differences in age, height, upbringing, religion and bank accounts, they were very happy together. St. Yves, with his deep family roots, and many years as a warden and on the Legislative Council, knew a great many people and had a good sense of what was what in Trinidad and Tobago. Sensing her desire to put down roots in Tobago, and to become part of the community around her, he must have been invaluable in advising Dorothy and setting her right, letting her know which of her ideas verged on the hare-brained and which had a chance of succeeding. Perhaps her boldest move, and one in which he would have been critically involved, was to run for elected office.

In 1953, County Council elections were held all over Trinidad and Tobago. They were still a novelty in the islands, as up to then the governor appointed by the Crown was the supreme commander, and bodies such as the Legislative Council, of which St. Yves had been an appointed member, served in a primarily advisory capacity. But colonial governments all over the world were starting to loosen the reins in what would be a slow journey from crown colony status towards full independence. The first County Councils, based on the system of local government used in Great Britain, were elected in 1946, a small step along this route, but in truth these councils had very little power and, again, could advise only. (This was the first election in which everyone could vote. Prior to this, suffrage was granted only to property owners, men over twenty-one and women over thirty, who could speak and understand English. This amounted to only six percent of the population.) By 1953, and the second County Council election, local councils were given executive powers. They had the authority to give financial assistance to village councils, for example, for the building of community centres and halls. They were responsible for the maintenance of local roads, cemeteries, recreation grounds, and markets. They oversaw abattoirs and public buildings, and the delivery of health and social services. All of this was done through the warden, who was now the chief executive officer of the County Council, instead of the direct representative of the governor, as previously. Tobago was a county of Trinidad and Tobago, divided into seven parishes, of which St. David, where St. Yves and Dorothy resided, was one. And it was here that she decided to register to be a candidate. The election would be held on February 2. Notices went up, in rum shops and markets, on walls and lampposts, all over St. David, listing the candidates and their various identifying symbols, so that those who could neither read nor write could make their choice with an X. Eight candidates put their names up for election in St. David: four proprietors, one cocoa dealer, a retired schoolmaster, a mason, and a housewife – Lady Dorothy de Verteuil. Her symbol was a heart. Other symbols were a star, a man's profile, a clock, an arrow, a wheel and a hat, all dwarfed by the outsized symbol of a hand with index finger pointing – the symbol of Alphonso Philbert Theophilus James. To oppose A.P.T. James in an election in Tobago would be for most political neophytes a gut-shrinking challenge.

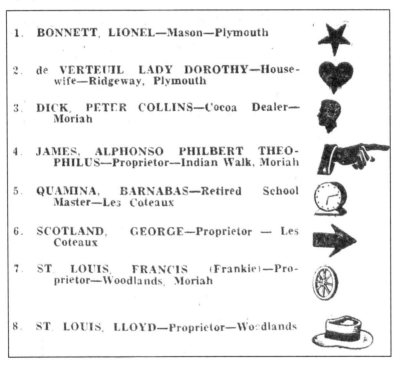

1. BONNETT, LIONEL—Mason—Plymouth

2. de VERTEUIL LADY DOROTHY—House-
    wife—Ridgeway, Plymouth

3. DICK, PETER COLLINS—Cocoa Dealer—
    Moriah

4. JAMES, ALPHONSO PHILBERT THEO-
    PHILUS—Proprietor—Indian Walk, Moriah

5. QUAMINA, BARNABAS—Retired School
    Master—Les Coteaux

6. SCOTLAND, GEORGE—Proprietor — Les
    Coteaux

7. ST. LOUIS, FRANCIS (Frankie)—Pro-
    prietor—Woodlands, Moriah

8. ST. LOUIS, LLOYD—Proprietor—Woodlands

List of candidates in the County Council elections, 1953,
Parish of St. David, Tobago

A.P.T. James was nicknamed Fargo because of his resemblance to the hefty British-made Fargo trucks used on the Pitch Lake in

Trinidad. Not only was he physically impressive, but he was known to have an unerring talent for crushing his opponents. He was colourful, charismatic, and a true Tobago man, a son of the soil. A.P.T. had been an elected member of the Legislative Council since 1946 (St. Yves had already retired from this body, so they probably did not know each other). He was a stevedore contractor, a union organizer and a clever businessman, owning several properties, one being a bar which he bought outright after he and some friends were refused service by a hapless bartender. There is now a park named after him in Scarborough, and a bronze bust of him on a plinth. He was the Apollo Creed, heavyweight champion of the world, to Dorothy's Rocky Balboa, the Goliath to her David.

Voting took place from 'seven in the forenoon' to five in the afternoon on Tuesday, February 2. The final count was announced that evening at the Warden's Office in Scarborough. The headline in the Port of Spain Gazette two days later read: 'Titled Lady Candidate defeats Tobago M.L.C.'. She had garnered 809 votes, to James's 600, the most votes cast for any candidate in Tobago, and Tobago had the highest percentage of votes cast in the entire colony. 'The applause was prolonged when the name of Lady Dorothy de Verteuil was announced'. She issued a statement thanking those who helped her and promising to do everything in her power for all the people. 'Her victory is all the more remarkable as she had no committee to assist her. It is believed that she received strong support from the women voters'. Only one other woman was elected in Tobago, Pearl Bailey, a milliner, in St. Paul. Dorothy and Pearl were among the first women to enter electoral politics in Trinidad and Tobago, and were true pioneers, breaking the ground that culminated in the election in 2010 of Trinidad and Tobago's first female prime minister, Kamla Persad-Bissessar.

How was she able to pull this off? In a newspaper article entitled 'Opinion of Titled Lady Candidate', Dorothy says that politics should be excluded from these elections (A.P.T. was head of the Caribbean Socialist Party), and that what is wanted instead is 'foresight, hard work and sound commonsense'. Candidates should not make wild promises. 'All one can say is that one will do one's best'. No other candidate in this election would have used the pronoun 'one' three times in a sentence. Dorothy spoke like an English aristocrat, with an accent that today would be derided as 'posh'. She was a large white woman, speaking in a manner unfamiliar to most of the voters in Tobago, and most certainly devoid of the common touch, the easy backslapping, joke-telling camaraderie possessed by most politicians. On the other hand, she was said to be completely without snobbery or any hint of racial bias. She had all the confident 'noblesse oblige' of an aristocrat, who in performing public service fulfills what is seen as a moral obligation to act with honour, kindliness and generosity. She and St. Yves were popular and deeply respected by the people of St. David.

But it's important to note that although this was the first time that Dorothy had run as candidate for an election, she was an experienced member of committees and boards of charitable institutions, and was by no means a neophyte at the essential political task of making speeches and knowing what to say to persuade a crowd, to get people to listen, and to appeal to them.

Two decades earlier, on November 11, 1933, she had been invited to chair the annual meeting, held in Glasgow, of the Lewis and Harris Association. Lewis and Harris is one island of the Outer Hebrides, eight times larger than Tobago but with only one quarter of its population. Dorothy and Rupert with their family and friends had gone there every year for eleven years in a row, to enjoy the fishing and sailing; but being Dorothy, she was not just a pleasure-seeking visitor but took a keen interest in the everyday lives and welfare of the islanders. To be invited as an outsider, not 'of the blood', to address their annual meeting was an honour indeed, and her speech in its entirety was published by the *Stornoway Gazette*. We can glean from it certain principles which she held dear. One was that 'it is all important that ... persons in a responsible position should constantly bear in mind the duties they owe to the community which looks to them to better conditions... At the same time, we are all becoming too dependent on our leaders ... and are apt to blame them for every misfortune that comes along ... the strength of the nation is in the individual citizens of the nation ... and the task of its leaders should be to apply that strength in the best possible way. People are too apt to think that when they exercise their vote they have elected someone to help to govern them and they are entitled to expect prosperity and happiness without other effort'.

This message of self-sufficiency is sweetened by her eloquent expressions of great love for the beauty of the island – 'there is a spot at the far end of Balallan from which, at sunset, the waters of Loch Erisort put the blue of the far famed Caribbean seas to shame' – and for 'the way in which time slips by one. There is never any hurry, never any rush...'. She is touched by 'the ruined church of St. Columba in Erisort, always sadder to me standing as it does deserted among the emerald green grass where the rabbits play around the stones that bear so many Island names'; this, from a mother who had buried her only son just the year before.

She ends the speech by noting that 'I am an Imperialist and I glory in the British Empire. But nowadays the units of this Empire have their own competent Governments and need no guidance or government from Home as they did in the old days when the Empire was young. What we want is for each unit of the British Empire to look after its own people and to remember that a great change has come over these people in recent years'.

There is no need to think that twenty years later her views had altered; they had matured and evolved, no doubt, but in essence remained the same, and the County Council elections in which she ran in Tobago in 1953 and so handily won were an important part of the 'great change' that she spoke about in 1933, a move towards self-sufficiency and full democracy for the people of Tobago.

I sat recently on the front porch of Joseph McDougall's neat house on Rabbit Lane in Plymouth on a breezy February morning, listening as he reminisced about Lady Dorothy and St. Yves, whom he remembered vividly.

Joseph McDougall in Plymouth, Tobago, 2020

He had known them well, having worked for them at Ridgway along with his brother Cyril. He told me of the real poverty in Plymouth in the '40s and '50s, when jobs consisted mainly of fishing for the men and market gardening for the women, occupations that his parents engaged in. Most people lived in what he called 'trash houses', made out of leftover bits and pieces, not the solid structures of today. Children were fed 'sweet water', a sugar/water mix, because milk was too expensive. Dorothy, he said, was exceptional in the way she dealt with problems faced by people in the village. Many people were helped by her. He mentioned in particular a man called Albert, pointing to his house down the road on Rabbit Lane. Albert was mentally disabled and indigent, and she was able to get him a pension to live on for the rest of his life. Everyone knew her, and he was not at all surprised that she competed successfully with

A.P.T. James in the election, because they saw her every day, and James, the politician, only came by during the elections. He said this with a 'steups', the classic sucking of the teeth used in the Caribbean to express mild derision. By 1946, only a few years married, she and St. Yves had fundraised enough money for a community centre in Plymouth, the very first in Tobago. Dorothy became chair of the Plymouth-Bethesda Community Council and held this position for many years. And on a private level, they often drove sick villagers five miles over the hills to the hospital in Scarborough, there being no doctor resident in Plymouth and no telephone. With no close family of their own nearby, they fostered several needy children, and were advisors and arbitrators in domestic and business disputes, a role that St. Yves was skilled at given his long working life as a warden. Before she had Ridgway built, Mr. McDougall revealed, she had already designed and built another house right in the village, on a scenic bluff with a wide view of the ocean. This she gave to the Plymouth community, to act as a house and clinic for the visiting doctor. He remembered St. Yves too. He had a deep voice and a thick neck, was stocky and solid, and always dressed in a crisp long-sleeved white shirt and tie. But she, he said, was the 'controller'. Mr. McDougall said that he maintained contact with Lady Dorothy right to the end of her life, when she had moved away from Plymouth to Scarborough. 'I never give she up'.

In looking back at Dorothy's remarkable work with the people of Plymouth, I think back to my childhood, and the car trips we took on a regular basis from our home near Arima to Port of Spain, to visit our grandparents, to the doctor, to have haircuts, to shop on Frederick Street, to meet up with friends. Parents went in the front seat of the family Ford Zephyr, windows wide open to maximize the breeze, with the rest of us piled into the back, 'fenning' the hotly contested seats near the windows. (To 'fen', a term derived from playing marbles, was to claim the right to a particular tactic.) The highway that took us into Port of Spain was bordered on the north side by Shanty Town, and on the south side by the city garbage dump, where the shanty dwellers foraged. We certainly noticed the smell of the dump, in the few minutes that it took to drive through this area, but the shanties themselves, the skinny children, the stray dogs, the strewn rubbish and the fetid streams bridged by pieces of scrap lumber were almost too familiar to notice. That is just how things were. Some people drove in motorcars along the highway, and others lived in Shanty Town.

To explain what made Dorothy think that she not only could but should do something about the poverty that she lived among in Plymouth, that 'from everyone to whom much has been given, much will be required' (Luke 12:48), one could reach back to her native London and the settlement movement, which was founded in the late Victorian period and peaked around the 1920s. Its goal was to bring the rich and the poor together, to have them live in close proximity. The volunteer 'settlement workers', often middle-class university students, would live in purpose-built 'settlement houses' located in poor areas. They would hope to share knowledge and culture with, and work to alleviate the poverty of, their low-income neighbours. This would be done through daycare, education and health care. It was the close proximity that counted, the everyday rubbing shoulders with each other, getting to know each other on a personal basis, rather than the orchestrated dropping in and out of a well-intentioned Lady Bountiful. Whether Dorothy ever was connected with the settlement movement in London is unknown, but it would certainly have been in the news and talked about in the charitable circles that she was part of. Could this have given her the inspiration and the model to work on a similar personal level with those in need around her?

Chapter 14

The de Verteuils learn to love Dorothy, corn-bird hat and all

When Rupert D'Oyly Carte died in his suite at The Savoy in 1948, Bridget was his sole heir. This made her a very rich woman indeed. It was natural that she would take his place as the head of the D'Oyly Carte Opera Company, and while not becoming president of The Savoy Group until later, she became a director, with a major responsibility for interior design. She was, like her mother, a pioneer, Dorothy in Caribbean politics, and Bridget in the corporate world of London, a world almost entirely populated by men. It was into her penthouse office at the hotel that the young Eric de Verteuil ventured, cap in hand. It was the early '50s, and he was a student in London, and broke.

The strained relationship between the de Verteuils and Dorothy and St. Yves had warmed considerably after Rupert's death in 1948, which had freed them to marry a second time in the Catholic Church. St. Yves first had to write a letter of apology for the scandal he had caused and have it published in the *Catholic News*. They were no longer 'living in sin', and from that time on, they visited freely back and forth with St. Yves's many siblings and their families. It must have been a great relief to St. Yves to be over this period of family sensitivity and to resume normal relations with his clan. So when his cheque from Trinidad was late in arriving, Eric had no qualms about going to see Bridget, having met her several times on her island visits to her mother. He was hoping that she could land him a job, any job, dishwasher, cleaner, it didn't matter. But when Bridget sat him down to hear his story, her response was swift: 'Hire a relative at The Savoy! Absolutely not'. But she softened this somewhat by slipping him a few pounds and inviting him to tea at her home near London, Shrubs Wood. (Eric subsequently got a job dishwashing at another hotel.) She had sold Coleton Fishacre after Rupert's death and bought Shrubs Wood, an architectural gem designed by Erich Mendelsohn and Serge Chermayeff. It is considered by architectural historians a major example of mature Modernism, a contemporary interpretation of the traditional English country house. It is set in twenty-four landscaped acres, surrounded by a further sixty-four acres of woodland. At Shrubs Wood she entertained many visitors from Trinidad and Tobago, among them of course St. Yves and Dorothy, who made several lengthy visits to England after the war and into the '50s. The names Salvatori, Du Boulay, Agostini, La Tour and de Verteuil are among the repeat visitors recorded in a leather-bound book now in Lord Cranbrook's archives.

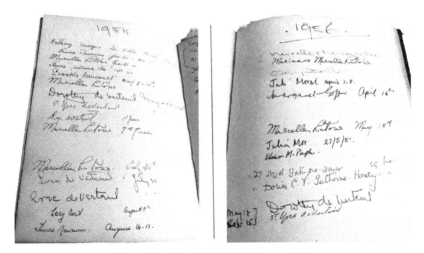

Pages from the Shrubs Wood guestbook

It is one of the few personal items that escaped the bonfire on her grounds at Shrubs Wood, lit by Bridget's gardener Frank at her request, shortly before she died of lung cancer at the age of seventy-seven. Letters, diaries, photographs, all thrown onto the bonfire, charred scraps floating into the autumn air. The guestbook was given to Bridget's friend, Jo Batterham, by the housekeeper Frances, Frank's wife, who thought it should be saved from the flames. One of the objects that Bridget held on to was a folded man's shirt which had belonged to a lover of many years, a well-known married man, who was very important to her and who had predeceased her. She asked for this shirt to be placed alongside her in her coffin.

Bridget was known to be very unassuming person, and despite her wealth and position, left-leaning in her opinions and her politics (she was a close friend of Labour Prime Minister Harold Wilson and his wife Mary). Had she not felt it her duty, after her brother's death, to join the family business, she would no doubt have continued her work in child welfare, for which she had a great affinity. She was also known to be very private and reserved, a quality she shared with her father, Rupert, but emphatically not with her mother. Dorothy was free-spirited and rather enjoyed upsetting convention. We can surmise, there being no concrete facts, that their relationship was strained by this stark difference in their personalities. Added to this was no doubt the natural resentment that even an adult daughter might feel at her mother's perceived abandonment. Dorothy was dealing with her own troubles when she decided to live in Tobago, but then so was Bridget. Her only sibling, Michael, had died tragically, her four-year marriage was over, she was dealing with a strong sense of sexual inadequacy, and her parent's marriage was on the rocks. Dorothy's departure could only have been an additional sadness for Bridget.

The penchant of the English aristocracy to engage in unconventional behaviour has been well chronicled. The Earl of Mar's favourite pastime was kicking pigeons. He lost his balance while doing this, and was found dead in 1975 underneath his London balcony. Dorothy on the other hand loved pigeons and in her later years would hold toast between her teeth for them to peck at while lying on her couch indoors. Dame Edith Sitwell, whose father Sir George lived on an exclusive diet of roast chicken and invented a revolver specifically for shooting wasps, had a unique style of dress described as 'an altar on the move'. She would not have been in the least put out at Dorothy sporting a hat made out of a corn bird's nest, which, hanging from a tree branch, looks like a long and very narrow basket. It's hard to imagine it as a workable hat, as there wouldn't be any brim at all to provide shade and it would instead cling to the head like a cloche, shedding twigs and little feathers. It would have been interesting to witness Bridget's reaction when she first saw her mother so hatted. Dorothy did not just wear the corn-bird hat in the privacy of her Tobago garden. It was on her head when, on board the French liner the *Antilles*, sister ship to the *Colombie*, young Kay Farmer of Tobago met her and St. Yves on deck. Kay says that in his way St. Yves, of medium height and smartly dressed, always seemed the more polished of the two.

Her ease with the animal world – always surrounded by dogs, taking pet mice to Harrods, wearing bird nests on her head, feeding pigeons from her mouth – led her to be an early pioneer in the battle to save the endangered leatherback turtle from poachers in Tobago. She was known to stay out on her own during the dark hours on Tobago beaches where the turtles were nesting, to protect them from those hoping to sell severed flippers in the market the next day. To be on a beach under the low-hanging stars while a leatherback, the largest turtle in the world, hundreds of pounds, is borne in on the waves to make its stately way out of the sea to its nesting site is to be a lady-in-waiting at a majestic ritual. There is no sound other than the steady roar of the waves, and there is no artificial light. If there were strange lights and sounds, the leatherback would stay waiting in the bay and the birthing would be delayed. Everything has to be in its place; the protocol has to be right. After it makes its ponderous way, huffing and panting, out of the waves and up the beach, above the tideline, there must be no touching of the behemoth, no unseemly closeness, no intruding flashlights. She does not fear the quiet presence of someone on the beach with her. Every impulse that she has is absorbed in the one great driving instinct of giving birth. She pays Dorothy no attention at all. Using powerful hind flippers, she digs a hole in the sand, about eighteen inches deep, and positions herself over it so that her hundred or so eggs, white and round and rubbery with a slight indentation on one side, can fall neatly, soundlessly, in groups of two or three. And while she does this, she weeps. Sandy, salty tears roll down her rutted cheeks, not from the pain of giving birth or the joy of returning to her own birthplace, but more prosaically, scientists tell us, to rid her body of excessive salt. After covering up the hole, scooping sand up with all four flippers as she moves in a circle, she tries to make the nest invisible by scattering sand in all directions, a vain task given the huge treads made by her weight. Now comes the moment in the ritual to majestically re-enter the ocean, which she does by pushing off the bottom until able to float. She swims away to the horizon, head bobbing among the waves, until out of sight of her lady-in-waiting, who by this time has been joined by St. Yves with a thermos of hot cocoa laced with brandy.

It is no wonder that by the time he was in his mid-eighties, St. Yves discovered a penchant for pipe-smoking in his comfortable slip-covered armchair in their shady front porch at Ridgway, happy to be more and more of an observer in the busy life of his energetic, younger wife.

It was there that Eric and Charmaine de Verteuil found him when they visited the couple in 1963 while on their honeymoon in Tobago. They had trouble finding a way into Ridgway, the arbour in front of the house being so thick with vines that Eric thought he might have to fetch a cutlass to hack their way in. Dorothy cooked them a roast-beef dinner using an old-fashioned wood-burning stove. There was a loaf of fresh bread, baked by her. Bare-footed Adolphus the butler served, and St. Yves smiled benignly, nursing his pipe and joining in with the occasional quote from Shakespeare. This would be the last time they would see St. Yves, who died shortly after at the age of eighty-eight. His grave is in the Lapeyrouse Cemetery in Port of Spain, part of the de Verteuil family plot.

Chapter 15

The Grande Dame of Tobago leaves but cannot stay away

When St. Yves died in 1963, Dorothy was seventy-four. Her friend, Kitty Alford, also widowed, became her personal assistant and companion. As you may recall, Kitty's husband, Commander Alford, was the author of the article about Speyside that had prompted Dorothy's first visit to Tobago in the 1933. He had also written a popular guidebook *The Island of Tobago*, and after his death Kitty edited the sixth edition, published in late 1963, with a short foreword by Dorothy. In it, she writes: 'So many changes have come to our island. Some, I am glad to say, for the better'. One of the principal changes that she is undoubtedly referring to is the independence of Trinidad and Tobago from Great Britain. At twelve midnight on August 31, 1962, the Union Jack was slowly lowered, and the national flag of Trinidad and Tobago, black, red and white, was unfurled for the first time. 'Trinidad and Tobago are now on their own. Looking ahead we expect this new nation to have greater prosperity, richer developments and world recognition as a nation whose people know so well how to live together harmoniously. We hope this new Independence will bring a feeling of personal responsibility for making Trinidad and Tobago a better place in which to live and work', Kitty Alford wrote in her guidebook.

The book fails, however, to mention in any detail the utter devastation visited upon Tobago by Hurricane Flora, which struck on September 30, 1963. The guidebook was about to go to press, and it was probably a wise editorial decision not to write about

Flora. Visitors were at the time wholly necessary to Tobago's small island economy, and it would not have been helpful to describe the damage that a severe hurricane can do.

Trinidad and Tobago lie out of the hurricane belt, situated as they are on the shoulder of the South American continent which extends a protective arm. But this time their luck ran out, and islanders were given two-hours' notice to prepare for the approaching cataclysm, heading due west from Africa. Hurricane Flora turned out to be one of the deadliest Atlantic hurricanes in recorded history, killing 7,193 people throughout the West Indies. I was working in Port of Spain at the time and was told to leave for home in Arima immediately. The winds were already so strong across the Churchill–Roosevelt Highway that they shifted my Volkswagen Beetle sideways back and forth across the road. I said the rosary, using the wavy bumps on the underside of the steering wheel as beads. Trinidad escaped with very heavy rain and fallen trees, the Northern Range of mountains protecting it from more serious damage. Instead, it focused its energy on Tobago. Blinding rain and winds of 193 kilometres an hour; towering seas up to seven feet above normal. Six large ships sank in Scarborough harbour, and the damage to the coconut, banana and cocoa plantations was so severe that they have never fully recovered.

The Tobago Main Ridge Forest Reserve, the oldest legally protected forest reserve in the world geared specifically towards conservation, became a graveyard of fallen giants. Established on April 13, 1776, the reserve was created by an ordinance which states that it is 'for the purpose of attracting frequent showers of rain upon which the fertility of lands in these climates doth entirely depend'. The passing of the ordinance is attributed to Soame Jenyns, a member of the British Parliament whose main responsibilities were trade and plantations. He was influenced by the ideas of the English scientist Stephen Hales who was able to show the correlation between trees and rainfall. It took Jenyns eleven years to convince Parliament that this was indeed a valid endeavour. Scientific American commented that 'the protection of Tobago's forest was the first act in the modern environmental movement'. Seventy-five percent of the trees in the reserve came down, resulting in the loss of animal and bird habitats. Of the 7,500 houses on the island, 6,250 of them were destroyed or damaged. Eighteen Tobagonians died.

This was the beginning of a difficult decade for Dorothy, newly widowed, living on a devastated island, with a shrinking group of friends, fewer of them returning to stay in the winters. Dorothy was approaching eighty, and both her arthritis and her eyesight were getting worse. And there were strange rumblings and disturbances afoot which were threatening to shatter the peace and security of island life.

Eight years after Independence, in early 1970, the Black Power movement, born and nurtured in the protests to the Vietnam War, in the fight against apartheid in South Africa, and in the Black Panther movement In the United States, made its way to Trinidad and Tobago, via Montreal, Canada. At Sir George Williams University (now part of Concordia University) in Montreal, several Trinidadians were among the ninety-seven students arrested and jailed, accused of causing property damage to the computer laboratories at the university amounting to two million dollars. They had been protesting against racial discrimination at Sir George Williams and the university's dismissive treatment of their claims. This incensed students at the University of the West Indies in St. Augustine, Trinidad, who, under the leadership of tall, dark and eloquent Geddes Granger (later Makandal Daaga) staged a protest march in Port of Spain to draw attention to the plight of the students in Montreal. The marchers decided to go into the Roman Catholic Cathedral in Port of Spain, where they draped two pale-faced statues, of the Virgin Mary and St. Peter, in black T-shirts. As Geddes Granger said, 'How could we be expected to worship in a church where we are not represented?' This proved to be an incendiary news item on the noon-time radio shows, and by that afternoon, thousands of supporters had come down from the hills of Port of Spain to join the students. The Black Power movement, as it came to be called, commanded the islands' attention for the period of February to April, 1970. As it matured, it changed somewhat. A series of orderly, peaceful, if noisy, marches gave way to ones hinting of possible violence, with broken store windows, the occasional Molotov cocktail and frequent clashes with the police; one of the young marchers, Basil Davis, was killed by the police during a demonstration, leading to a revitalization of the movement. The marches spread to Tobago; protests were staged at the Pigeon Point Beach, privately owned by friends of Dorothy, the La Tour family, and run as a tourist facility, accessible only to those who bought tickets. The marchers were incensed that they were barred from swimming at their own island's beaches, and when stopped by a phalanx of police, responded by hoisting the ticket gate right out of the ground and throwing it into the sea. They then stripped down and dove, in hundreds, into the pristine turquoise waters. They also protested closer to Plymouth, at the Mount Irvine Golf Course. How unjust it was, they felt, that a place like that, so green and luxurious, could have all the water it needed for the golf greens, when the nearby village of Bethel had a water supply that was intermittent at best. They also marched the many miles from Scarborough to faraway Charlotteville, and the island resounded to the chant of 'Walk, black man, walk!'

Bridget, away in London, was well informed of what was going on in Trinidad and Tobago. Like everyone else, she read the papers, but she would also have had direct access to the inside information and wisdom of her friend the prime minister, Harold Wilson. He could well have advised her that it was time for her mother to leave Tobago and move back to England. No-one could predict how the political situation might play out. As it turned out, the Black Power leaders, including Geddes Granger, were eventually arrested and confined when a state of emergency was declared in late April, but there was the additional drama of an army mutiny, which was unsuccessful but revealed the ambitions of some Trinidadian army officers to stage a Cuba-style revolution. The place was in turmoil, and tension was high. There were armed guerrillas in the hills, and frequent police stops and searches along the highways. Dorothy finally gave in to Bridget, who was understandably concerned about her aging mother's welfare. Dorothy was living in what was starting to look like a very different place from the one she had moved to thirty years before. With regret, Dorothy sold Ridgway with her beloved garden, gave away her library of over two thousand volumes, dispersed her possessions and said goodbye to her friends, the villagers of Plymouth and the remaining Brethren. By 1970, she was back in England. Her set of majolica ware, with the initials SYDV and DDV intertwined, went up for sale at McLeod's, an antique store in Port of Spain. I couldn't afford the whole set and tried without success to interest Mr. McLeod in parting with a dish.

Her relocation to England was not a success, however, and by 1972 she was back. We don't know exactly why, but one can guess that she had lived in Tobago for too long and had become too rooted there to try to fit in again to life in England with Bridget at Shrubs Wood. As well, Bridget had relocated for part of the year to a castle in Scotland, Barscombe, owned by Sir Hugh Wontner, the managing director of The Savoy Group. She was helping him to renovate it, and loved being there and the simple life it offered. But for an arthritic octogenarian like Dorothy, the cold stone steps of Barscombe leading from the lower floor to the only bathroom upstairs must have been challenging, not to speak of the damp and often gloomy weather of Scotland.

Her return to Tobago was eased by the calming down of the political situation. It turned out to be a lot less destabilizing than originally thought, and particularly in Tobago, life continued much as before. Because Ridgway had been sold, and her possessions dispersed, Dorothy spent her last years in a rented, furnished apartment near Scarborough, at the Castle Cove Beach Hotel, with a view of the ocean, simple accommodations that her friends thought "beneath her station." She was welcomed back and featured in a full-page article in the *Trinidad Guardian*, headlined 'The Grande Dame of Tobago'. In the photograph accompanying the article she is holding forth from her daybed, phone propped next to her on a pile of books, sans pigeons.

She was to spend much of her old age propped up by pillows on this daybed, phoning her friends and talking into a borrowed tape recorder. She could no longer write letters easily because of her eyesight and the poor state of her handwriting, and so she sent cassette tapes to Bridget instead. Sadly, they are often indecipherable recordings, with an excess of ambient sound, roosters crowing, pop songs blaring on the radio. The Tobago breeze alone would be enough to muffle her low voice with its cultured English accent. But what can be heard tells of an old age full of spirit and without a trace of self-pity. She is keenly observant of the limited world around her. She tells amusing stories of her childhood, and of local, everyday happenings. She was looked after by Camilla Allowsing, after Kitty's death. She and Camilla would fly over to Trinidad occasionally, where she stayed either with St. Yves's niece Adie de Verteuil on Dere Street, or at the Queen's Park Hotel. She enjoyed playing bridge and betting on the horse races at the Queen's Park Savannah. Friends threw a birthday party for her, which started after the horse racing was over. Featuring rum punch and cake, it went to 8.45, and presents included bottles of cologne, brandy and boxes of soap. She found the pigeons rather haughty when she first got back to Tobago, but they soon started flying in again for their crusts.

Dorothy at Castle Cove feeding pigeons c. 1975

She could no longer move around with any ease and relates with delight that a big tall man, Mr. Crooks, picked her up like a baby when the plane landed in Tobago and lifted her down the airplane steps. She comments on local politics as a loyal citizen, using 'we' and 'us' instead of 'they' and 'them'. She is taken aback by the misuse of public funds, a thirty-foot sea wall taking one and a half years to build at a cost of $200,000. She's interested in her friends' welfare: someone's had an operation, someone else is as thin as a rail; she's lending a Madeira cardigan to her friend Sybil who is travelling to America and will be cold. She loves the quiet at night, and the curious yellow light, harbinger of rain the next day. She shells peas with Camilla, which bores her, and dines on peanut butter and honey on brown bread, with a large cup of very hot Frye's cocoa. She saw Albert Gomes, the politician; she'd last seen him in Geneva many years before. He has written a book which she wants to read, on the early days of the aborted Federation of the West Indies. He has lost a great deal of weight, having been enormously fat when he was in government, and is married to a charmingly pretty wife who looks about twenty-two. After hearing of the death of old Mr. Charles, who might have survived had there been an available supply of oxygen at the local hospital, she will write to the Minister of Health to remonstrate. A new couple has moved in across the way; they have their own furniture. Camilla thinks they are government officials. 'No doubt we will get to know them'. The couple before them were prisoners of the Japanese through the last war and have moved to Barbados where there is greater opportunity to take walks. An old Arabic Jew who only writes in Arabic has lived since 1931 in Tobago, having worked with the British Army. She had fought successfully on his behalf for a pension, when she became aware that he was living on black coffee, bread and rice. He came to thank her, knelt on the floor with his hands on his head and burst into tears. 'I felt so embarrassed I didn't know what to do'. Eric Williams, the prime minister, is a perfect autocrat, a very clever man. She drinks blended brandy (only nine dollars a bottle) every night as a cocktail. She doesn't believe in women's equality. 'They'd be far happier if they would stay home and look after their husbands' [she, one of the first female politicians in the islands, referring to working women as 'they'!]. There's some place in America where everyone lives on honey to a very advanced age. She doesn't want to live that long. Maybe eighty-eight. That was the age that St. Yves was when he died, and that would be quite enough.

Her wish was fulfilled. She died on February 21, 1977, at the age of eighty-eight. Her old friend Josset Legh was still on Pigeon Island but would die one year later, at the age of ninety, on her only trip back to England since the war years. Dorothy's grave is in the public cemetery in Plymouth, adjacent to the community centre that was built with funds she raised in the mid-1940s, a simple building, solid as a rock. She was buried under a flamboyant tree, next to her friend and neighbour Edith Cook, who also was witness at her marriage to St. Yves in the Warden's Office. Dorothy, I gathered, would have preferred a 'watery grave', that is, to be buried at sea, but my source said that such a burial is hard to arrange and so this plan was abandoned.

Dorothy's grave in the public cemetery, Plymouth, Tobago

As it was lowered, the gravediggers blessed her coffin with a good dose of Trinidad rum and then finished the bottle. Some old friends in Plymouth were left money by her to see to her gravestone, which they decorated with black and white six-inch bathroom tiles. The tiles are falling off now, and the etched name on the tombstone is hard to read: Dorothy de Verteuil née Gathorne-Hardy. The pink blossoms of the coralita vines grow wild and thick, and tethered goats feed among the gravestones. She would have liked that.

Addendum I

Trip diary

Volume upon volume, twenty in all, of the first Lord Cranbrook's diaries were found after his death in 1906. He had shared them with no-one, and didn't think much of them, said his son Alfred, who fortunately disagreed with his father, and edited and published two volumes[1] of annotated diary excerpts, which provide an account of the day-to-day life of an extraordinary man, involved, energetic, and intellectually engaged until the end of his very long life.

In the entry for Monday, April 13 (1885), he writes, 'With a thankful heart I record that all is well here (GC) [gratia Christi] when we arrived on Saty afternoon.... The West Indian trip is chronicled in a separate book taking in the period between Feb 2 & April 12 & it was without a drawback'. This 'separate book' has unfortunately never been found, but before her death Dorothy gave a typewritten copy of it to her friend Tom Cambridge, who then gave it to Eric de Verteuil. It is a record of a trip made to the West Indies in 1885 by then Viscount Cranbrook, with his son Stewart and wife Cicely, Dorothy's parents, and Dorothy's eldest sister, Nina. He was at the time in opposition, and while constantly in touch by telegram with what was going on at Westminster, he could afford to be away for several weeks.

The first entry on arriving in Trinidad on Friday, March 20, is written from Governor's House, Port of Spain. 'The water began to lose its grand ocean tint of purple and deep indigo ... probably

---

[1] Gathorne Hardy, First Earl of Cranbrook, *A Memoir with Extracts from Diary and Correspondence*, edited by the Hon. Alfred E. Gathorne-Hardy, two volumes, Longman Green & Co., 1910.

owing to the violence which the Orinoco pours into the Gulf beyond Trinidad. We first sighted the mountainous outline of Venezuela on the starboard side, and Trinidad appeared faintly on the left with islets between. ... Many porpoises had amused our course with their antics and wonderful display of speed as they kept alongside through water so clear that we could watch them like living shafts that pierce the moon. ... The entrance by the gates of the Boca nearest the islands was very fine and the beauty of the scenery of these lake-like bays with Scotland islets was most remarkable. The Dragon Mouth is certainly an admirable entrance to Port of Spain and the inhabitants appear to avail themselves of the various islands for small villas and bathing resorts'.

The governor at that time was Sir Arthur Havelock, who had very recently taken up this post.[2] His launch fetched them, and there was some initial embarrassment at his inability to put them all up, owing to the fact that he and Lady Havelock had not even unpacked. Cicely and Nina were found rooms at the Hotel de Paris in downtown Port of Spain, while Gathorne and son Stewart spent the night at Government House, an airy, wood and stone two-storied building tucked against the hills of St Anns and fronting onto the wide green expanse of the Savannah, next to the Botanical Gardens. 'This house is on a grand scale for receptions, but scanty in bedrooms. The Ballroom is 75 ft. by at least 35 ft. It stands in the Botanical Gardens, with wonderful examples of trees and shrubs, many with magnificent blossoms and strange fruits.... Stewart has been out early with the Curator whom he has found pleasant as well as instructive, and who has given him many specimens and seeds

---

[2] Sir Arthur was fresh from West Africa and Liberia; prior to that, he had served in various capacities in Mauritius, the Seychelles, and Fiji. His stint in Trinidad was for only one year; he and his wife Anne, Lady Havelock, would go on to serve in Natal, Zululand, Ceylon, Madras and Tasmania, before he took early retirement, citing ill health brought on by too many years in the tropics. And exhaustion, no doubt; his schedule seems grueling for even the most robust Victorian. He died in 1908 aged 64.

for experiment at home'. They joined Cicely and Nina at the Hotel de Paris the next day, which he gives a mixed review: 'Our quarters here are rather public and promiscuous,[3] but the food is good and the beds are clean and comfortable, so that we have no right to complain – the accommodations are not of a high order, but I have experienced worse on the continent many a time. The Bath is excellent in water but gloomy and damp, with no place to put anything down, and the walk to it only suitable to the tropics if that'. The week spent in Trinidad included a drive to the Blue Basin, the route taking them by a large 'coolie'[4] village, where they made some purchases of jewellery: 'It is astonishing what a fortune for them they carry on arms, ears, noses and legs. The husband of one would not let his wife sell her bracelets at the sum she would have gladly taken for them, but put an extortionate value on them'. It was a beautiful drive, 'through the lowlands, hills on our right, masses of palms, cocoa trees and fruit trees of all descriptions and blossoms which were new to us. Plenty to beguile our attention, to keep our eyes open... A steep ascent, and descent conducted us to the circular pool below surrounded by steep rocks, which is called the Blue Basin. The epithet may at some time be thus described but neither the water or the locality were of cerulean blue. Still, it is a charming locality and the vegetation hanging around being tropical, gives it an air of peculiar beauty, while the dash of water falling from a height of some 40 ft. is delightfully refreshing'. But as every tourist knows, these side trips cost money, and Lord Cranbrook notes that 'the bank shut at 12 so I failed to improve my exchequer, which is of no great importance, as I have enough'. The week in

---

[3] 'Promiscuous' is used here not in the modern sense of 'having many sexual relationships', but rather in the old-fashioned sense: 'of mixed and disorderly composition or character' (Oxford English Dictionary).

[4] Coolie is a dated term, used in this context to denote an indentured labourer from India. It is now considered derogatory and offensive.

Trinidad filled out with leisurely drives around the Savannah 'by many a bright villa with its brilliant shrubs and flowers, not to say anything of trees. The cotton silk ones … amaze us by their grandeur in magnitude and form but I fear they are all show and of little service. The Savannah plain extends to the very base of the noble hills which rise very abruptly from it. …nothing could exceed the beauty of the hills and plains and sea, and the multitude of palms of all sizes and kinds through and over which we looked on the extended ocean … and these islands of the blest'. On Sunday they went to the Trinity Cathedral for service at eleven, 'a sermon not notably preached by an unexcited gentleman of placid demeanor and curious dialect which had a savour of Wales'. And of course, a trip to the Pitch Lake by boat, with a side trip into San Fernando, 'a clean little town with new churches and new looking houses not many in number. … The situation is pretty as a conical hill rises there in company with a small brother of the same shape'. A boat took them to La Brea, where their host Mr. McCarthy had 'extemporised a wooden pier to land and reembark us dry and that was a great benefit as there was a good deal of wave. La Brea is a village of pitch employees and has its R.C. and English churches and a Government School which many children appeared to be attending cleanly and orderly as far as one could judge'. The visitors were then put on five chairs in a cart drawn by mules 'over all manner of excrescences and ups and downs' which made for a 'case of pitch and toss'. 'Pitch is everywhere but nowhere defiles, you may take it dry or moist and nothing sticks to your hands. Men with planks to cross the rifts of translucent water, which traverse the pitch surface were ready at every needful point and made our progress easy. It is a strange scene – at first the surface is hard and firm – then it takes a faint impression, and gradually creeps over until you meet the centre of liquid matter where the water is turpid and sulphureous, and you see it boiling up as if from a murky spring. The pitch rises to fill up what is dug out and the store is unfailing as the widow's cruse…. This seems a supply for ever. I do not enter into causes but suppose some bituminous forest passed to render this useful substance which finds a market in all parts of the world, for roofs, pavements and lawn tennis courts etc. etc. … There are islands in it with luxuriant vegetation and the drive or drag to the sea through groves of palms of all kinds some of which were new to us – trees of varied fruit and flowers. There was an avenue of Cashew nut trees all the way to the lake … the nut must not be cut lest the sap blister your skin, but be roasted before it is dealt with. In that state the nut is considered a great delicacy and is certainly very good. We bought some bottles of them'. On the following day, Lord Cranbrook was rewarded with a 'glorious sleep in my bed, a good bath', an early morning visit to a gentleman's club to read the newspapers, and then to the bank. They visited a sugar estate near St. Augustine in the afternoon owned by a Mr. Agostini, who he says deserves praise for 'all the new inventions and economic processes' introduced to his Usine [sugar refinery]. 'We visited his new hospital, where they were a few patients. A coolie has been hurt while we were there. He showed no signs outwardly of injury but his moans and bewailings seemed rather over the occasion. However he is the best judge poor fellow of his own suffering'. Their stay continued with visits to St. Joseph – 'an ordinary little town, or village, but plumes itself on having been the Capital, and I believe the Spanish element in race and religion is strong there. Indeed Romanism is in the ascendant in the Island, and the patois of the black is French and not English, although the latter is generally understood'. He found the openness and airiness of tropical architecture not to his taste: 'Houses in this climate are easily run up, and the word comfort is hardly applicable to what must be free to the winds of heaven, and proof to the rays of the sun. It is the comfort of these fiery regions to find such resting places but other words would better express the feeling. For instance the construction of the public room is quite suitable to its use, but comfortable or cosy would be singularly inappropriate description of its complete publicity'. Maracas Falls gave rise to 'many an exclamation of surprise and delight'. 'We made our way through many a ford, over a bright rocky brook with water beautifully transparent, by splendid feathery bamboos of great height, undergrowth of wondrous luxuriance.... The Falls have much to recommend it ... a fall of some 400 feet and I expect that there is a cascade or torrent in the wood above the precipice over which it comes in sheer descent.... The valley ends abruptly in a rocky recess beneath the Falls and the hills rise with masses of trees, among which the yellow blossoms of pouis were ... conspicuous, and very effective in contrast'. After all this exertion, the group was ready for 'the dejeuner, which our coloured followers spread on vast plantain leaves for a table cloth decorated with bright flowers of which they had gathered a bouquet in the centre'. He disappointingly does not tell us what they had to eat, other than oranges, freshly gathered and deftly peeled, 'that the skin might not irritate our lips'. The next day – Santa Cruz, up through the Maraval Valley, through shady bamboos arching the road, and a visit to Sir Joseph Needham's cocoa plantation. 'The views were very lovely from his terrace walk, and we saw growth in all stages. When this was done we went back half a mile to a picnic in our honour and were warmly welcomed by people who seemed bent on pleasing. A good dinner and dancing followed, and then a charming drive home in brilliant moonlight'. And so ends 'pleasant Trinidad and its hospitable folk, some of whom will see us aboard'.

They met an extraordinary number of people while there, not surprisingly, given Trinidad's penchant for socializing and the novelty that a party such as the Gathorne-Hardy's would have provided. The governor and his wife, the Havelocks, of course, with their party: the Maryatts, Agostinis, Bakers and Warners. They were entertained by our great-great aunt, Elisa Cadiz Warner, second wife of Charles Aucher Warner, who had been attorney-general of Trinidad for many years, and who was in 1885 a gentleman of 80, 'courteous and friendly with the kind of talk of a past day interlarded with quotations in Latin and English, not inappropriate. He was animated about politics in which he represents the good Tory school'. They met a Mr. Oakley, and a countess something or other ('of doubtful fame'), Judge Fitzgerald, Mrs. Walter Russell and Captain Jackson. And while mention is made of 'negresses … dressed … in their best … such gorgeous colours mingled in a harmonious contrast seemed not unsuited to the ebony complexion' and of Indians, always referred to as coolies: 'They are a handsome race with a certain dignity in the face, but oh what spindle shanked men they all are', they are never called by name, other than a jeweller Alibocas, commissioned by Cicely to fashion some earrings. We are aware as we read this trip diary of the many invisible people around the English party, driving mules, peeling oranges, carrying and serving picnics, building temporary ramps across the Pitch Lake, preparing baths and cleaning hotel rooms. But given Viscount Cranbrook's reputation as a kind and generous man, one imagines that those trips to the bank meant good tips for these invisible people; and the lack of mention of the names of those who serve is not limited by any means to people of colour. He was a man of his time and of his class, and in his entire long diary, kept in several volumes and covering most of his life, Lord Cranbrook rarely mentions servants by name. The one case that stands out is when a drunken footman, Woolworth, drove a carriage so recklessly that one of his lordship's grandsons fell off and into a pond where he nearly drowned. Unsurprisingly, Mr. Woolworth is mentioned once, and then no more.

Cicely always kept a bowl of flamboyant seeds in her living room as a memento of Trinidad; no doubt, when the young Dorothy asked about them, she was told about this memorable family trip in 1885. The curator of the Botanical Gardens gave these seeds to her father, Stewart, during their early morning stroll through the Gardens, when he acquired many specimens for experiment back in England. Cicely's enthusiasm for Trinidad, and the fact that Dorothy had the trip diary in her possession until she died, suggests that these 'blest islands' held a very special place in Gathorne-Hardy family lore.

Addendum II

Dorothy's homes

Coleton Fishacre, Rupert and Dorothy's country home and gardens on the coast of Devon in England, is now owned by the National Trust for Places of Historic Interest or Natural Beauty, commonly known simply as the National Trust. It has been open to visitors since 1999. Although very little in the way of furnishings survived from the time of the D'Oyly Cartes, it has been beautifully furnished, after much research, in the style of the 1930s, guided by a 1930 Country Life article on the house. I was interested to see that in the information given to visitors, Lady Dorothy marries for the second time a Count St. Yves de Verteuil, of an illustrious Trinidadian family, and her new title is Countess de Verteuil! Poetic license, perhaps?

Ridgway, the house that Dorothy built on the hill near Plymouth, Tobago, has been sold twice and remains, eighty years later, in excellent condition. It survived Hurricane Flora admirably, due to the high quality of its concrete and stone walls, the heavy galvanize from Jamaica used to roof it, and the ceilings of mora wood from Guyana. The gardens are rich with sapodilla, tamarind, pommerac, cashew, caimite and Julie mango trees, whose fruit attracts a visiting agouti. There was a Ruby-topaz hummingbird at the feeder when I visited.

Addendum III

Dorothy's will

Lady Dorothy, daughter of a rich aristocrat, independently wealthy, and married to a man of considerable resources, died with $3,561.79 TT in her Barclays bank account, and $681.55 TT worth of furniture. The value of the Trinidad and Tobago dollar is at the time of writing around $6 TT to $1 US.

In her will, dated November 22, 1972, shortly after she returned to Tobago, she bequeathed all the contents of her rented apartment at Castle Cove to her executor, Robert C. Johnson, a retired diplomat and friend. After the payment of funeral expenses, six months' wages was to be paid to her housekeeper, Rosa Kelth, if she was still in her service at the time of death, all other money going to the Tobago Branch of the Society for the Prevention of Cruelty to Animals.

She had enjoyed her wealth to the full, and she died with very little left of it, owing in no small part to her signature generosity, both to public causes and to personal friends. One example is buying the lifetime lease of a 40-acre Caribbean island for her friend Josset Legh. There were also many small gifts, things of all sorts, a tapestry here, a fine piece of china there, books, jewellery. On one of her initial visits to Trinidad in the 1930s, she presented the museum in Port of Spain, The Royal Victoria Institute, with five oil portraits of former Governors of the Colony, and gave a fine pair of vases to the tiny St. Peter's Church which sits on the sea at Carenage.

To own so little when she died suggests that she worked it all out ahead of time, and realizing that her end was near, she kept just enough to see her through, sparing her executor the task of disbursement. Should Dorothy's calculations have been a bit off, and she had lived much longer, Bridget, her wealthy daughter, was but a phone call away.

Acknowledgements

This book would never have come into being without the help of many generous people.

In Tobago, I owe thanks to Alex and Jennifer de Verteuil, for many conversations and introductions, and for reading the first draft; Kay Farmer and Joseph McDougall (who knew Lady Dorothy and St. Yves); Randall Rostant, current owner of Ridgway; and for so generously sharing her deep knowledge of Tobago, the historian Susan Craig-James.

In Trinidad, Eric de Verteuil answered numerous emails with patience and humour, and provided photographs and anecdotes; and I drew extensively on the work of his twin brother, Father Anthony de Verteuil, the prodigious and respected historian, for all details on the history of the de Verteuil family. Ann Dardaine helped greatly with research in newspaper archives.

In England, the Gathorne-Hardy family, through Simon and Harriet Fraser, have supported the project and were very generous in sharing information and photographs. I was introduced to them by Alan Powers, architectural historian. I am greatly indebted to them, and to Lord Cranbrook, for his permission to use his great-grandfather's trip diary. Josephine Batterham and Louise de Ville Morel provided very useful background, based on their friendship with Bridget D'Oyly Carte. The National Trust staff at Coleton Fishacre were very helpful in allowing me access to their files. I am indebted also to Dame Marina Warner and to Christine Lalla for reading the final draft and for their enthusiasm for the project.

In Canada, Kathryn Willms has been a godsend, patiently editing the manuscript and seeing it through the process of self-publishing.

Finally, I am grateful beyond measure to Leslie Topp, Bob Topp, Anna and Anthony Luengo, Wendy Bonus, Jean Ferguson, Sylvia Topp and Patricia Stelzner, for reading the first draft and for their support and encouragement at every turn. Thank you all.